25-5-99
99p
D0505478
DIGITATIONS

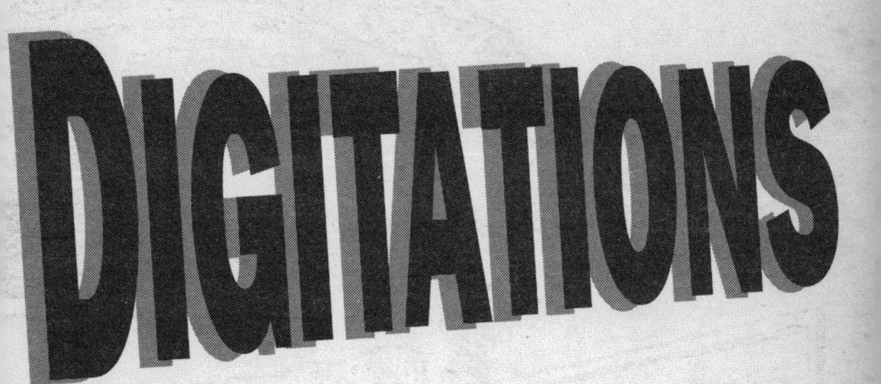

A Battery of Mind-Blowing Number Crunchings from the Cutting Edge of Eco-Paranoia

ROWLAND MORGAN

Michael O'Mara Books Ltd

This edition first published in 1996 by
Michael O'Mara Books Limited
9 Lion Yard, Tremadoc Road
London SW4 7NQ

A CIP catalogue record for this book is available from the British Library.

ISBN 1-85479-632-1

Designed and typeset by Robert Updegraff
Printed and bound in England by Cox & Wyman, Reading
This book is printed on paper made from sustainable resources

Author's Note

This is not a systematic reference book, but an anthology. Citation of a source does not mean the digitation is an excerpt. Some are, but most are original insights calculated and written by the author drawing on the sources cited and additional research. For the entries that are reproduced verbatim, grateful acknowledgment is hereby extended to the authors. Throughout the text, the arrogant official term 'England and Wales' is always changed to the more gracious 'Wales and England'. Contributions are gratefully considered; readers wanting to send digitations should address them to the author at the publisher's. Access to references can usually be obtained by asking the sources for Boolean searches on their databases using keywords. The type of paper used in production is the responsibility of the publisher. This collection is available on disk and can be purchased with all the advantages of instant hypertextual search, for £12.50, including postage and packing by sending a cheque or money order to: Digitations on Disk, WONC Ltd, PO Box 248, Twickenham, England TW1 3DG.

Specify format: 3.5" IBM format....3.5" MAC format.

Please allow three weeks for delivery.

Measures

Supertanker 100,000 tonnes

Semi-trailer truck 23 tonnes

Road tanker 30 tonnes, 50 ft long

Olympic swimming pool 2,300 cu m

Football field 1.33 acres

Euro-barge 3,000 tonnes

Introduction

Here is a fresh collection of digits for meditation – 'digitations' is a word I coined for them for a regular column in The Guardian Weekend. You don't have to be a rocket scientist to enjoy making these calculations: I only got a grip on mental arithmetic by playing darts in the pubs around The Lanes in Brighton. It's a long-standing newsroom knack which I developed after the Vancouver Sun hired me as a reporter and the first wire story I had to rewrite was headed The British Breakfast Causes Cancer. A newshound in New York had number-crunched all the dietary horrors of coffee, bacon, sausages, eggs and butter and used them to flash doom round the globe and sell papers. Not long after, our Gaelic-German news editor, Patrick Nagel, handed my copy back with the note: 'Beef-up nose with numbers in par five' and using a cheap (non-recyclable) pocket calculator I picked up the trick of turning civil servants' predictable statistics inside out to brighten up a story. A shining example to me was Sun columnist Bob Hunter, the first president of Greenpeace anywhere, who was blowing all our minds, dishing up the new breed of calculations; things like the tonnage of lead being dumped by car exhausts, or the whole forests of trees being felled. The environmental issue became an eruption of amazing numbers.

Now we inhabit a world in which the biggest feature is no longer a bomb or a pill, but a number: the imminent doubling of our human population to 10 thousand million. True, you could stand all 10 billion in the county of Devon (with less than a square yard each), but to enjoy the fairly cramped density of

the British population they'd need the whole of Asia. On the other hand, spread out over the five continents, they could be as bucolically distributed as the French. And if we somehow forgot about cities and industrial hard labour, and wandered around dressed in skins having a permanent picnic, like our later-paleolithic ancestors, research has shown that we could all be unemployed and only have to 'work' collecting food for an average of three hours a day, taking frequent naps.[1]

Unfortunately, 10 billion people speaking 5,000 tongues are not likely to share out the five continents into football-field lots of about 14,000 square metres each, however sensible it would be. (Those receiving a piece of the Sahara could rent it out for solar power, and if you got one of the Himalayan peaks you could probably sell the water.) The problem is, less than 2 per cent of our human bodyweight is brain – we're really not as bright as we think we are. I suppose the 600-odd calculations in these troubled pages go to prove it. Some genius worked out that 100 deep laughs are a better work-out than 10 minutes' hard sit-ups. So, dear readers, try to see the funny side of all this – it could save your life!

Eel Pie Island,
River Thames,
England

1 Marshall Sahlins, Stone Age Economics, London 1974.

Would You Believe it?

As well as Bill Gates, boss of Microsoft, America has another 202 known billionaires.

Michael Tobias, Environmental Meditations, Freedom, California, 1993

Nearly nine out of 10 Germans live in an energy-guzzling urban environment, with a fossil-fuel-burning car for every male in the country. (86.5 per cent, 37.6m cars)

World Resources 1994–5

Indians use 73 kilos of commercial fertilizers on a hectare of cropland, Germans use half a tonne.

World Resources, 1994–5

While Germany's population has remained stable over the past 60 years, Great Britain's has increased by 13 million, or 30 per cent.

Britain's population in 1938: 44.5 million. In 1992: 57.75 million. Germany's in 1938: 81 million. In 1992: 81 million.

Whitaker's Almanack, 1939 and 1995/Eurostat

Every year, the British government gives 52 times more aid to the 95-year-old Labour Party than it does to all the lepers in the world.

Government aid to the Labour party per annum: £1,426,709. To the Leprosy Mission: £27,419.

Parliamentary Fees Office (the Short Fund)/Overseas Development Agency, Hansard, vol. 267, no. 5, col. 46

Rockets launching satellites have ripped a gash in the Earth's protective ozone layer on average once every four days since 1957.

Known successful satellite launches: 3,400. Approximate tonnes of dangerous hydrogen chloride emitted around the ozone layer: 119,000.

Royal Aircraft Establishment/The Observer (est 35t HCl per launch)

Long before they got an explosion of bad publicity by resuming underground tests at Mururoa Atoll, the French government exploded more than 40 nuclear bombs in the atmosphere over inhabited South Pacific islands.

Le Journal du Dimanche

Every week, Britain's biggest daily newspaper groups alone use enough forest-sourced newsprint to load a queue of semi-trailer trucks 10 miles long.

BZW estimate/UKPG no. 1500 (1.28m t (not including the Guardian group), semi-trailer truck 23t)

Although it is frequently wrong, and failed to predict Britain's Great Storm of October 1987, the UK Ministry of Defence's weather forecast costs £350,000 each working day.

Hansard, vol. 246, no. 135, col. 631

Annual crops of fruit, vegetables, pasta and wine from sunny Spain and Italy have been sprayed with nerve-gas-based pesticides as heavy as 28 Eiffel Towers.

Annual tonnes of pesticides used in Spain: 134,000. In Italy: 91,000.

Tonnes of metal in the Eiffel Tower: 8,757.

Species of insect, including major pests, which have developed resistance to chemical pesticides: 500.

Joni Seager, The State of the Environment Atlas, Penguin 1995/Quid 1995/The Ecologist, September–October 1991

German households are at least 15 times better connected than British.

Households with cable TV in Germany: 13,900,000.

Households with cable TV in Great Britain: 908,000.

Cable News Network

Germany has at least one dead lake killed by pollution for each 11.5 square kilometres of its forest and woodland.

Dead lakes in former East Germany: 9,000.

Sq km of forest and woodland in Germany: 40,000.

Dr Volker Beer, cited in Worldwatch Paper 99/The Information Please Environmental Almanac

It takes German civilization just 101 days to emit the weight of the Great Pyramids of Cheops in major climate-changing pollutants.

Estimated tonnes of major climate-changing pollutants emitted per day in Germany: 69,000.

UK Department of the Environment

Every day, western Europe's newspapers use nine articulated road-tankers of hard-to-recycle ink.

Olympic swimming pools of non-soya inks used by Western Europe's newspapers in 1993: 195. (97,500 t)

Frost and Sullivan

Europe will kick off the new millennium with a store of toxic nuclear fuel waste which could load a 20-mile semi-trailer traffic jam.

(Semi-trailer truck 23t; fuels of varying danger levels).

Tonnes of nuclear fuel waste expected to be in storage Europe-wide by 2,000: 48,000.

J. Donaldson et al, Management of Used Nuclear Fuel and High Level Nuclear Waste in Europe, 1994 Centre of Environmental Chemistry, Brunel University, 1994

If the Chinese adopt western flying habits, the country will have 17 million polluting airliner movements a year, averaging over 46,000 a day, or 32 per second.

Air transport movements for 57 million Britons at UK hub airports 1993–94: 871,407. Times the People's Republic of China's population exceeds Britain's: 20.

British Airports Authority plc, annual report

Percentage of persons in the 1995 Birthday Honours List cited for services to English literature: 0.14. (2 in approx. 1,500)

The Prime Minister's Office

There's nowhere to run to: even travelling at the speed of light, it would take 1,300 years to reach the first known planet outside our solar system; at the speed of sound, it would take about 10 trillion years.

Distance in miles from Earth to first known Milky Way planet: 7,700 million million.

Alexander Wolzsczan, University of Pennsylvania/
Philadelphia Inquirer, 26 February 1994 (1,300 light years)

Japan has twice as many industrial robots as the rest of the world put together.

Industrial robots in Japan: 274,210.

In the USA: 41,304. In the UK: 6,418.

In all leading competitor countries: 107,619. (end of 1990)

'Japan 1994, An International Comparison'. Keizai Koho Center, Tokyo, Japan

More than 40 per cent of CFCs (stratospheric ozone-depleting fluorocarbons) now in the atmosphere will remain after 100 years.

Yearly percentage increase of CFCs in the atmosphere now: 2.

Sherwood Rowland, University of California, Irvine, quoted in The Washington Post

When a typical mortgage taken out next year expires, more people will have been added to the world population than existed on the planet in 1933.

US Census Bureau's latest estimate of world population: 5.6 billion. Expected in 2020: 7.9 billion. World population in 1933: 1.993 billion.

New Scientist, no. 1924/Whitakers Almanack, 1939

For every job created in the industrialized world, 12 must be created in developing countries.

The 1994 Information Please Environmental Almanac (USA)

Chemical companies eagerly anticipate a quadrupling of Asian nerve-gas-based herbicide sales within six years.

Annual sales of food crop herbicides in China and India: $67 million. Expected by 2000: $550 million.

New Scientist no 1924

Tobacco costs half as much in Italy as in Britain, but Italians only smoke 10 per cent more.

Amount spent on tobacco in Britain in 1994: $17.78 billion. In Italy: $8.67 billion.

Cigarettes per capita: UK 1,409; Italy 1,552. Cigarettes manufactured in the EC each working day: 23 million.

Euromonitor: Consumer Europe, 1995

A line of articulated lorries loaded with the amount of sulphur dioxide belched annually from the coal power station at Boxberg, (East) Germany would stretch three kilometres. (198 lorries @ 23t)

Dr Volker Beer, cited in Worldwatch Paper 99

France sells nearly twice as much to Germany as Britain.

Value of British manufactures exported to Germany per year: $21,010 million. Of French manufactures exported to Germany per year: $36,483,000.

UK Department of Trade and Industry

Number of chemical, biological and nuclear weapons allowed Germany by its Treaty of Union: 0. Number of British Chemical and Biological Defence Establishment personnel visiting US Pentagon germ and chemical warfare laboratories 1992–93: 56.

The Economist/CBDE/HM Treasury

Aerial bombardment in the Gulf war for oil was greater than that delivered by Britain's Royal Air Force against Nazi Germany.

Tonnes of bombs dropped on Germany by RAF during World War II: 970,369. Tonnes of bombs dropped on Iraq and Kuwait by US coalition: 1,080,000.

Iraqi children estimated killed by typhoid resulting from destruction of power supply for water: 350,000.

Christy Campbell/BBC TV News and Current Affairs/Harvard Medical Team

The French recycle twice as much glass as the British.

Tonnes of glass recycled annually per 1,000 population in Britain: 5.6. In France: 13.

The Grocer

The British are in three times more pain than the French.

UK sales of analgesic pain-killers per year: $307 million (up from $211.5 the year before) France's: $85.3 million.

Euromonitor: European Marketing Data and Statistics, 1994 (1992)

Radio is 14 times more centralized in Britain than in Italy.

Radio stations in the UK: 181. In Italy: 2,500.

UK Radio Authority/Campaign magazine

Putting non-renewable fossil fuel in a car is nearly four times cheaper in the USA than it is in Germany, and over three times cheaper than in France.

Average price of a litre of car-fuel (non-diesel) in France: $1.11. In Germany: $1.17. In the USA: $0.30.

Worldwatch Institute ($1.11 US gal)/Quid, 1995

Since environmental awareness started spreading, far from conserving energy, French people have increased their energy consumption by 50 per cent.

Per capita energy consumption in France in 1991: 160 gigajoules. Percentage increase since 1971: 51.

World Resources Report 1993–4, Washington DC

Italy's rail subsidy is nearly four times Britain's.

Taxpayer's annual rail service subsidy per route mile in Great Britain: £93,750. In Italy: £348,000.

UK Department of Transport (£1.5 billion for 16K miles in 1994–95)/Ibid (1990 figure inflation-adjusted to 1995)

France has twice the population of Kenya and 77 times the global warming carbon-dioxide emissions from industry.

Eurostat/World Resources 1994–5

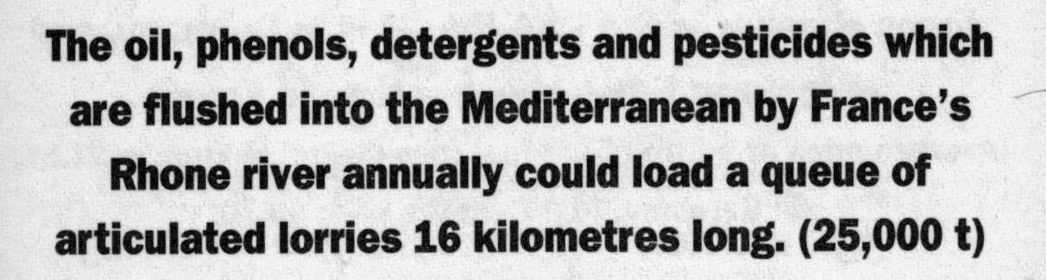
The oil, phenols, detergents and pesticides which are flushed into the Mediterranean by France's Rhone river annually could load a queue of articulated lorries 16 kilometres long. (25,000 t)

Earthscan

France conducted atmospheric nuclear tests at a five times higher rate than China.

Atmospheric nuclear test explosions conducted by France in Polynesia 1966–74: 44, or 5.5 per year.

By China in Sinkiang Province: 1964–88: 22, or 0.9 per year.

International Physicians for the Prevention of Nuclear War

Would You Believe it?

Britain has 14 times Spain's submarine nuclear strike power.

Nuclear-powered nuclear-war submarines owned by UK Ministry of Defence: 14. Nuclear-powered nuclear-war submarines owned by Spain's Ministry of Defence: 0.

UK Department of Defence/Jane's Fighting Ships

The world's salinating irrigated lands could accommodate five Spains.

Professor Viktor Kovda, University of Moscow

Germany has 38 per cent more people than Egypt and nearly 12 times the global-warming carbon dioxide emissions from industry.

Joni Seager, The State of the Environment Atlas, London, 1995

An average of 320 exotic birds are imported into Germany every day, and 334 exported from Guinea in Africa.

CITES

France has about the same population as Egypt, and nearly 50 times as many cars.

American Automobile Manufacturers' Association

Tobacco consumes nearly eight times its own weight in forests, because around 7.8kg of wood are needed to cure 1kg of tobacco.

Tobacco: The Smoke Blows South, Panos Institute, London 1994

Britain fought World War II with the same number of telephones as are now registered on the cellular network.

Cellular registrations 1994: 3 million.

Telephone stations 1937–38: 3 million.

British Telecom/Whitaker's Almanack, 1939

Britons are consuming nearly 4,000 Olympic swimming pools of diluted sugar as soft drinks a year. (9,000m l, Olympic pool=2.27m l)

The Grocer

Half the three billion people in Asia are under 25.

Number of them murdered by police in Tianenmen Square, Peking: 500.

The Hongkong and Shanghai Banking Corporation Ltd, advertisement/Focus magazine (estimate)

The same number of UK jobs now has to support 5.5 million more people than in 1959.

UK employees in employment in 1959: 20.99 million. In 1993: 20.99 million. Increase in population 1959–93: 5.5 million.

Employment Gazette, vol. 102, no. 10 (from pop. 52.5m to 58m)

Britons have half as many computers as Americans, and 134 times more than Indians.

Computers per 1,000 population in the USA: 265. In the UK: 134. In India: 1.

Lester R. Brown et al, State of the World 1994, Worldwatch Institute, Earthscan

Of every five barrels of oil the world produces, two are used by Americans.

Percentage of world oil consumption that is used by the USA: 40.

Worldwatch Paper 84, Worldwatch Institute, Washington DC

Only 10 per cent of humanity can afford to buy a car, while 80 per cent can afford a bike.

Worldwatch Institute, Washington DC

Rich countries have about 24 times more blood for transfusion than poor ones.

Average units of blood available per 1,000 people in most industrialized countries: 50. In developing countries: 2.2.

World Health Organisation/Panos Institute, World AIDS, 32

Estimated number of rickshaws in Dhaka: 200,000.

Daily earnings of a Calcutta rickshaw puller: $1.

Roushan Zaman, Panoscope, 38

The world's poorest billion inhabitants receive 1.4 per cent of all global income, the world's richest billion, 83 per cent.

Warren Lindner, Connections, UNED-UK Spring 1994

Young Frenchmen do a total of more than 2,000 centuries of military training a year.

Approximate number of youths draughted for 10 months' military service in France each year: 265,000.

Quid, 1995

France has more than twice as many cinema screens as Britain.

Cinema screens in France: 4,821.

In Britain: 1,848. World cinema screens: 89,000.

New Scientist (1992)/UK Department of the Environment/Carnegie Mellon magazine

A high school in Seine-Saint-Denis, France, counted 54 nationalities among its pupils.

Paris Match

The current life expectancy of the world's biggest forest is just 30 years.

Square kilometres of Siberian forest felled illegally per year: 90,000. Square kilometres felled legally: 20,000. Sq km of England: 130,000.

Professor Alexey Yablokov, Royal Institute of International Affairs/
The Hutchinson Guide to the World, London, 1994

The production of 11,000 unnatural man-made organochlorines now exceeds 40 million tonnes a year, or the weight of 770 Titanics.

Johnson and Macrea, Death In Small Doses, Greenpeace International 1992/ Quid 1995 (Titanic 52,000t)

It would take pollution inspectors about 85 years to visit all Britain's factory premises.

Premises regulated by the Factory Inspectorate: 540,000.

Inspections by HM inspectors of pollution 1991–92: 6,327.

Department of the Environment, Health and Safety Executive/ Department of the Environment, Hansard, vol. 211, no. 51

Only one UK household in 1,162 showed interest in helping the Earth.

Coupon replies to the British government's, 'Helping the Earth Begins at Home' advertising campaign: 19,520.

UK households: 22,698,000.

Department of the Environment, Hansard, vol. 238, no. 59, col. 715/ Eurostat, Luxembourg

Would You Believe it?

For every one of Queen Elizabeth I's subjects, Queen Elizabeth II has more than 11.

Estimated English population in 1570, based on the number of baptisms, burials and marriages: 4,160,221.
In 1991: 48,069,000.

Whitaker's Almanack, 1994

25,000 Barbie dolls are sold every business hour. Laid head to toe, they would span 10,000 miles per year. It would take only 18 years of production to string a line of them to the moon.

Number of Barbies each little girl living in the world could have today: 6. Sales of Barbie dolls per second: 2. Per year: 63,072,000. (6-day week, 8-hour day)
Inches per Barbie: 12. Miles to the moon: 221,463.

Mattel-Corgi

A potato has more chromosomes per cell than a human being.

A potato's chromosomes per cell: 48.
A human being's: 46.

The Hutchinson Dictionary of Science, London 1994

The Soviet state used atomic bombs as excavators 116 times.

National Geographic, vol. 186, no. 2

A single piece of paper folded in half 32 times achieves a thickness of just over 271 miles.
(4.3m sheets @ .004" thick)

Independent on Sunday

Britain's imports of kerosene run higher now than during the massed invasion of Nazi Europe.
UK litres of kerosene imported in 1944: 1.67 billion.
In the latest year: 2 billion.

*CSO Business Monitor Dec. 1991 Table 111/CSO Fighting with Figures

Making PVC for bottles, window frames, sheeting, etc., produces enough poisonous dioxins in Europe alone to supply everybody on Earth with more than the maximum annual dose.

Greenpeace/J. Emsley, The Consumer's Good Chemical Guide, W.H. Freeman, 1995 (WHO standard)

Every year, nerve-gas-based pesticides outweighing 15 Titanics are spread over Europe.

Kilograms of pesticides distributed annually per European: 1.58.

Eurostat (793,759 tonnes)/The Hutchinson Guide to the World (pop. 500m)

Since the first weather satellite was launched in 1960, Britain has lost enough permanent meadows and pastures to fit into a million football fields.

Eurostat: Europe's Environment Statistical Compendium (13,000sq km lost 1960-90; football field 2.7 acres)

A million tons of pulsar stars would fit into a thimble.

Information Please Almanac, 1992, New York 1991

Polluting herbicides, based on wartime nerve gases, are 10 per cent cheaper now than they were in 1990.
(other than those containing phenoxy derivatives, acetic acid, etc)

Central Statistical Office Annual Abstract of Statistics, 1995

Over the past decade, the US federal government has spent $53 billion enforcing drugs laws, locking up 260,000 people in the process.

New Scientist, vol. 143, no. 1945

The USA's prison population is set to outnumber its current fourth-largest city.

US prison population: 925,000. Annual rate of increase: 6.5%. Expected in 2005: 2 million. (1993; percentage from mid-1991)

US Bureau of Justice Statistics

US officials spend half a million dollars a day investigating drug-dealers' guns.

Budget of Bureau of Alcohol, Tobacco & Firearms for drug-related firearms investigations: $137,900,000.

US Budget, Office of the President

Nearly eight times more blacks than whites are sent to prison in the USA.

Imprisonment rate per 100,000 US blacks: 1,534. Per 100,000 US whites: 197. White Americans among the 95 million O.J. Simpson trial TV audience who thought he was guilty: 75%. Blacks who thought he was innocent: 73%.

Dr Steve Whitman, cited in New Statesman and Society/ Broadcast/Independent On Sunday

O.J. Simpson's murder trial lasted over 8,000 times longer than an Old Bailey trial in Britain's Victorian heyday.

Average minutes' duration of an Old Bailey trial in 1833: 8.5. Minimum minutes' duration of the Los Angeles murder trial of footballer-turned-actor O.J. Simpson: 75,000.

V.A.C. Gatrell, The Hanging Tree, OUP, 1994/Reuters

455 bus-loads of debtors were imprisoned in 1993, a traffic jam over four miles long.

Male Welsh and English debtors imprisoned: 51,047. Female: 2,663.

Hansard, vol. 239, no. 71, col. 892 (50ft)

The average UK 16-year-old has tried three illegal substances.

Cannabis convictions in 1993: 42,000. Per working day: 161.

British Medical Journal, no. 6963, vol. 309/University of Exeter/Simon Jenkins, The Times

Britain's bicycles are stolen at a rate of 34 an hour.

Bicycles reported stolen in the UK in a year: 222,242.

Today, 31 August 1993 (1992)/London Cyclist (18-hour day)

Ninety-seven out of a hundred stolen bicycles are never returned to their owners by Greater London's Metropolitan police.

London Cycling Campaign Action Bulletin, December 1994

The British police use 12 tonnes of ozone-layer destructive CFCs per year for developing fingerprints.

Date of the Vienna Convention for the Protection of the Ozone Layer: 1985.

Police Scientific Development Branch/New Scientist, no. 1949/
The Earth Report 3, London 1992

One-third of all Welsh and English men born in 1953 had been convicted of a 'standard list' offence by the time they were 31 years old.

HM Chief Inspector of Constabulary annual report, 1992

The British police intend to store enough computerized fingerprint records to cover two out of five adult males.

Non-retired male adults in Britain: 18.4 million.

Fingerprint records to be held on the police computer: 7 million.

Whitaker's Almanack (1994)/
HM Chief Inspector of Constabulary annual report, 1992 (NAFIS database)

An American is 18 times more likely to murder than a Briton.

Murderers among 100,000 young British men: 1.2.

Among 100,000 young American men: 22.

Statistical Abstract of the USA

Handgun ownership in the USA has quadrupled since 1960.

Handguns in the US in 1960: 16,000,000

In 1970: 27,000,000.

In 1989: 66,700,000.

Erik Larson, Lethal Passage (USA)

There are 30,054 tribally-appointed lay magistrates in Wales and England.

Lord Chancellor, Hansard, vol. 238, no. 58, col. 619

There are just 334 male Texans over 20 years of age per Texas gun store, and an average day sees more than three people shot from a moving vehicle in San Antonio.

Time magazine/The Times

About 480 handguns are owned in the USA for every one owned in Wales and England.

Handgun certificates held in Wales and England: 138,400. US handguns: 66.7 million.

Home Office/Handgun Control Inc, Washington DC

In the USA a violent crime occurs every five seconds.

Crimes of violence per year in the USA: 6 million.

Firearm thefts every year: 38,000.

Wall Street Journal

In 1992, 3,336 Americans under the age of 19 were murdered with guns, and 1,429 used them for committing suicide.

Handgun Control Inc, Washington DC

There are 103 handgun murders in the USA for every one in Canada, and 400 for every one in Britain.

1992 handgun murders in the USA: 13,220.

In Canada: 128. In the UK: 33. In France: 42.

All Wales and England homicides by shooting: 72.

FBI Uniform Crime Reports/Home Office.

Even 60 years ago, US homicide figures were 70 times greater than Britain's.

US homicides in 1936: 10,200. UK homicides: 145.

FBI Uniform Crime Reports/Whitaker's Almanack for 1939

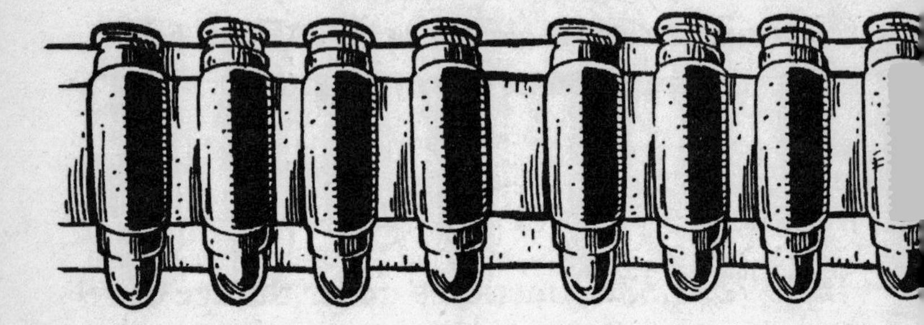

Gunshot deaths of youngsters in the USA outnumber US battle casualties in Vietnam.

US under-19s killed by guns 1979-91: 50,000.

US battle deaths in Vietnam War: 47,382.

Americans under the age of 19 killed with firearms each day: 15.

Handgun Control Inc, Washington DC

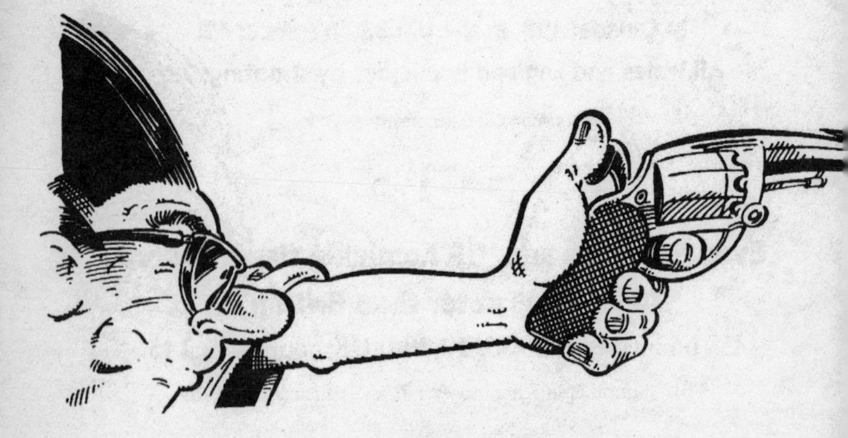

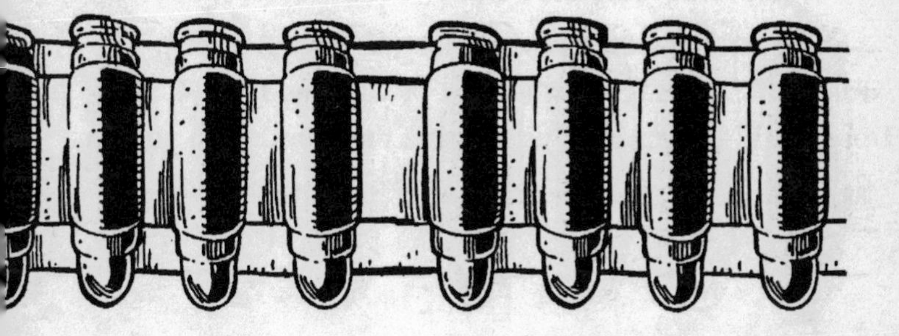

Californians, who have small penises, purchase 489,000 guns per year.

Guns bought in greater Los Angeles in the 11 days following the April 1992 race riots: 20,578. Average centimetres of erection among 85 men in San Francisco: 12.8.

San Francisco Chronicle/
University of California at San Francisco study, cited in New Scientist, no. 1976

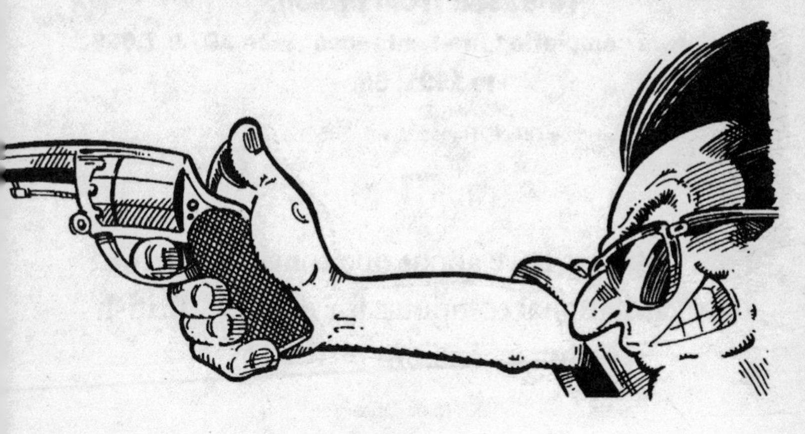

British officials make an average of 34 major seizures of illegal drugs a day.

Kilos of MDMA (Ecstasy) seized by customs 1993-4: 500.

Doses of 'E' estimated to be entering the country: 45 million.

Richard Spring MP, Hansard, vol. 242, no. 97. col 930 (9,000 in past year)/ UK Home Office

Dover's anti-smuggling checks were cut by 25 per cent in two years.

Anti-smuggling customs staff years in 1991: 280. In 1993: 208.

Home Office, Hansard, vol. 236, no. 36, col. 353

Each week in Britain a murderer is released from prison.

Murderers completing life sentences since 1972: 1,068. In 1991: 56.

Home Office, Hansard, vol. 235, no. 25

Police officers have about one conviction record on their national computer for every 13 British adults. (3.956m in 1992)

UK Home Office

Britain's prison population could be cut by nearly one-fifth if the Home Secretary exercised powers to cut long sentences by six months.

Disturbances in prisons in 1985–6: 38. In 1993–4: 147.

Home Office, Hansard, vol. 242, no. 98, col. 669 (9,000 out of 48,225)/Hansard, vol. 242, no. 97, col. 626

There are 20 times as many cannabis convictions now as there were in the year abortion, contraception and homosexuality were decriminalized.

Cannabis convictions in 1993: 42,000. Per working day: 161. Simon Jenkins, The Times (1967)/1988 British Crime Survey

Percentage of violent incidents which involve a drunken customer of the booze industry: 44.

Simon Jenkins, The Times (1967)/1988 British Crime Survey

If unconvicted prisoners in Scotland paced the length of their cell half the time they were locked in it, they would walk 43 miles a week.

Daily hours in cell target for unconvicted Scottish prisoners: 18.
(cell=12ft, 1 ft per sec)

Hansard, vol. 244, no. 112, col. 244

An estimated 222 million assorted firearms are privately held in the USA, enough to arm 32,000 Wales and England police forces.

Firearms officers on 34 forces out of 43 in Wales & England: 6,769.

Guided missiles procured by the US Pentagon 1989–91: 228,235.

National Rifle Association/Aerospace Facts and Figures (USA)/
HM Inspector of Constabulary

Judges' lodgings cost the English public £14,000 per working day.

Lord Chancellor, Hansard, vol. 242, no. 93, col. 243

Babies born inside Welsh and English prisons in the last 10 years: 691.

Hansard, vol. 244, no. 112, col. 252

Families have to travel an average of 75 miles to visit youths in closed young-offender institutions.

Average miles travelled to visit women prisoners: 62.

Prison trainees: 82.

Hansard, vol. 244, no. 112, col. 252

One-sixth of all prisoners are inhumanly crowded in accommodation that costs £1,024 a week.

Number of prisoners in Wales and England: 48,225.

Number of prisoners sharing two-to-a-cell designed for one: 8,500.

Target average cost of a prisoner per year: £26,624.

Home Office press office/Hansard, vol. 244, no. 112, cols. 274 & 244

Over £1 billion a year could be saved by releasing UK prisoners into community service.

Average monthly net operating cost per prisoner: £2,019.

Per community sentence: £106.

Hansard, vol. 244, no. 112, col. 272

Offenders get away with more than four out of five crimes reported in Greater London.

Reported crimes per year: 944,185. Cleared up by police: 150,946.

Metropolitan Police Commissioner's Annual Report 1992–3

UK prisons now have six times more lifers in them than when the notorious Kray Twins were imprisoned.

(1:70 in 1970/1:12.5 in 1990)

UK Home Office

Items of fan mail received since his conviction by John Wayne Gacy, part-time clown and murderer of 33 American men and boys: 25,000.

The Economist vol. 331, no. 7863

There is one police officer per 401 Britons, but one black or Asian officer per 1,742 members of ethnic minorities.

Whitaker's Almanack 1994/HM Chief Inspector of Constabulary annual report, 1992

Although one-in-three men get a record, fewer than one-in-20 government investigations of companies result in the disqualification of a company director.

DTI company investigations under the Companies Act since 1970: 82.
Directors disqualified as a result: 4.

Business Age, 41

Spending on security guards (sometimes criminals themselves) in the UK more than doubled in the four years from 1990 to 1994.

Expenditure on security guards in 1990: £303 million. In 1994: £695 million.

Business Age, 39

Black or Asian officers are nearly as rare in the British police as male homosexuals in the population.

Total police strength: 128,045. Officers of colour: 1,730. Ratio of blacks or Asians in police: 1:74. Of gay males in the population: 1:90. (male partner in last 5 years)

HM Chief Inspector of Constabulary annual report, 1992 'RM' Wellings, Kaye et al, Sexual Behaviour in Britain, Penguin, 1994

The Lord Chancellor spends 10 times more on portable phones to run the courts than the Serious Fraud Office does to keep check on the whole of British business.

The Lord Chancellor's annual bill for portable and car phones: £151,308. The Serious Fraud Office's: £14,560.

Hansard, vol. 244, no. 111, col. 149, & col 171

One policeman in seven in the UK is assaulted every year, but two members of the public are hurt in traffic accidents per policeman.

Assaults on police (usually during arrest) in 1992: 18,497. England & Wales police strength: 128,045 Road accident casualties in 1993: 306,020.

HM Chief Inspector of Constabulary, annual report 1992/Whitaker's Almanack

Prosecuting double-murder suspect O.J. Simpson for one day cost five times more than a whole UK pollution prosecution.

Average cost of one day's prosecution of Simpson: £38,000.

Average cost of a prosecution by HM Inspectorate of Pollution: £7,000.

Time, vol. 146, no. 3 (92 days/$5.6m to May 31)/Dept of the Environment, Hansard, vol. 260, no. 109

It costs £81,000 ($130,000) a year to hire a national police officer in Britain.

Police officers on the National Criminal Intelligence Service: 248.

1993–4 cost of NCIS: £20.068 million.

Home Office, Hansard, vol. 260, no. 109

The cost of fitting out MI5's new secret-police headquarters at Millbank, London, could have built an Olympic sports stadium and staged in it an international athletics event costing £40 million.

Cost of preparing Thames House as security service HQ: £227 million.

Of Manchester's proposed Olympic stadium: £187 million.

Home Office, Hansard, vol. 235, no. 26, col. 339/Building magazine

Food Fight!

A German spends nearly twice as much on food as a Briton.

Average Briton's annual spending on food: £766.
A German's £1,453.

Hansard, vol. 239, no. 68, col. 605

The flour used at a pizza restaurant chain for one year's pizzas weighed the same as seven jumbo jets.

Marketing Week (Pizzaland)

Raw materials used to support the world's most profligate lifestyle for a year could fill a line of supertankers from London to Sydney.

Earth Island Journal (USA)

The UK's biggest supermarket chain expected its 1995 sales to increase at a rate of nearly £2,000 a minute.

Neighbourhood corner shops which could be fitted into Tesco selling space: 34,000.

Average days between openings of new Tesco supermarkets: 14.

Tesco plc (£1,000m)/Farmers Weekly, vol. 121, no. 11 (350 sq ft shops)/Hansard, vol. 247, no. 140, col. 362

The proportion of Britons grocery-shopping only once a week has nearly tripled in 20 years.

Percentage of people grocery-shopping once a week in 1975: 31. In 1993: 86.

Mintel, Consumer Habits/The Grocer

Food now travels 50 per cent further from field to mouth than it did in 1978.

SAFE Alliance/Geographical, November 1994

Food travels three per cent further from field to mouth each Xmas.

SAFE Alliance/Geographical, November 1994

In the past century fat in chicken meat has increased by 1000 per cent.

International Journal of Biochemistry, New York, 1970, pp. 295–305/
James Goldsmith, The Trap, Macmillan, 1994

British chain-shops make up to three times as much profit as their nearest continental rivals.
Marks & Spencer's percentage operating profit margin: 13.4.

Marketing magazine

A production line of goods for Americans packed in see-through plastic packs would stretch two million miles.(21.7bn @ 6in)

Predicast Forecasts (USA)

Americans use 100 times as much synthetic chemicals as they did when they joined World War II.
Supertanker loads of synthetic chemicals produced in the USA in 1940: 11. In 1992: 1,078. (2.2bn lb to 214bn lb)

Earth Island Journal (USA)

An American uses 60 times as much water as a person in Ghana – and a resident of Las Vegas in the Nevada desert uses 10 times more water than a rain-soaked Londoner.

Croissance magazine/Time magazine

An American will use 40 road-tankers of oil in his or her lifetime.

The Economist Intelligence Unit

An American discards about four times his or her weight in product packaging every year. (600lbs)

Information Please Environmental Almanac

A food multinational found it used 85 different additives to make its 'ice cream'.

Unilever/SAFE Alliance

An estimated 15 per cent of all food sold in the USA gets binned.

D. Pimental, Waste In Agricultural And Food Sectors (USA)

Potatoes are 100 times more expensive as crisps than in their natural state.

Price of a pound of potatoes at the farm: 3.6p ($0.06)

Price of a pound of potatoes as Golden Wonder crisps: £3.78 ($6.00).

Donation to charity made by Coke-owned Walkers Crisps for every £7,274 it profited: £1.

Food Miles, SAFE Alliance (@ 25p per 30g packet)/New Covent Garden Market/ A Guide to Company Giving, 1993

Americans rubbish 132 supertankers of compost food waste every year, nearly equal in weight to the entire annual wheat production of Britain.

US Environmental Protection Agency

Transporting a year's sugar supply for Americans would take a traffic-jam of semi-trailer trucks stretching the length of Europe from Cherbourg to Athens.

Number of toothbrushes a year recommended to be thrown away by US dentists: 1 billion.

US Department of Agriculture (8m tons; 3,400mi)/The Natural Choice (US advertisement)

More than half of all English women are fat or overweight.

Percentage of women who said they had bicycled during the 30 days before survey: 6.

The Health Survey for England/
Central Statistical Office, Social Focus on Women

Britons eat more than a million tonnes of canned food a year, or a stack of cans about 170,000 miles high, which it would take an airliner three weeks to fly up.

Euromonitor: Consumer Europe

Europeans could eat half the meat they do, and still eat more than the prosperous Japanese.

Euromonitor: European Marketing Data and Statistics

Britons eat 451 million cans of baked beans a year, 224 times as much as Europe's second-largest consumer, Sweden.

The Independent

Every hour, five American consumers injure themselves with a supermarket trolley.

Seriously overweight Americans: 1 in 5.

Americans sent to hospital emergency wards by accidents involving supermarket trolleys each year: 33,000.

US Consumer Product Safety Commission/US Center for Disease Control

Of one hundred latex condoms used during heterosexual intercourse, four break.

Survey cited by Dr R.C. Noble, Professor of Medicine, University of Kentucky/ Newsweek

One in every 100 American men carries the Aids virus.(Estimates put the female rate at 1/800)

BBC News & Current Affairs (1992)

One in four young women now leaving school will have had an abortion by age 25.

The Times

Women who smoke have more lovers.

Percentage of women who had more than four lovers in the last year, and who smoked: 70.

Percentage of women who had no partners in the last year, and who did not smoke: 60.

New Scientist, no. 1910

A phallic lift costs less than a face lift.

Price of a hydraulic penis and handpump: £2,700 ($4,450).

Price of a face and neck lift: £3,612. ($5,600)

Focus/San Francisco Chronicle

An estimated 400,000 child prostitutes in Thailand are infected with HIV.

Estimated child prostitutes in Thailand: 800,000.

Estimated percentage with HIV: 50.

WorldWatch, vol. 7, no. 4, Washington DC

Percentage of Pakistani couples using artificial contraception: 10.

New Scientist, no. 1943

In Kampala, Uganda, where one girl in three aged 15–19 tests HIV-positive, aid agencies supply men with an average of eight condoms a year.

Panos Institute, WorldAIDS, no. 38

83 per cent of US high school students do not use Aids-protection during sexual intercourse.

Indiana Department of Education, 1990 (condom use)

A typical ejaculation of human semen contains five calories of nutrition – and a ton of danger. (Unprotected fellatio is now only recommended within lifelong, faithful marriage).

The Kinsey Institute

Ten million children are expected to have Aids by the year 2000.

World Health Organisation

Russia expects 20,000 Aids cases a year. Aids cases predicted by the Russian Aids Centre for 2000, from close to nil in 1995: 100,000.

The Guardian

An authoritative estimate says nearly half of all US women have had high-risk sexual intercourse anally; another says 40 per cent of them enjoyed it.

Kinsey Institute 1990 (40 per cent; other surveys varied down to 20 per cent)

US teenagers are exposed to about 14,000 items of TV sex smut every year.

N. Postman, Entertaining Ourselves To Death

Heterosexuals are reckoned to make love 142 times more often than is necessary for reproduction.

Average sexual acts in a lifetime: 5,000.

Sex acts considered necessary to conceive 2–3 children: 30-40.

Focus magazine

About one in a hundred sexually active couples prevent conception by abstinence.

K. Wellings, et al, Sexual Behaviour in Britain, Penguin 1994

Nearly half the heterosexual couples in the world do not use artificial contraception.

The Independent

At any given moment, about 2,300 people are starting to make love – and share body fluids.

Number of times per day people make love world-wide: 100 million. Resultant pregnancies: 1 million. Resultant abortions: 150,000.

World Health Organisation/
Michael Tobias, Environmental Meditations, Freedom, 1993 (USA)

Men claim to have penetrated more than twice the whole available female population.

Basic number of women penetrated by UK men who claim to have penetrated more than 10 women ever: 33,540,000. Available British women between 16 and 60: 14,210,000.

Anne M. Johnson et al, 'Sexual Lifestyles and HIV Risk', Nature, vol. 360, no. 6403/Whitaker's Almanack

A woman's orgasmic potential is eight times a man's.

Orgasms measured in an hour on a woman volunteer: 134.

On a man: 16.

William Hartmann, Center for Marital and Sexual Studies, California, USA/Focus magazine

Sexually active British women who have never had an orgasm could populate the cities of Birmingham and Manchester.

Frigid sexually active British women: 1,421,000.

The Full Treatment, (programme supplement) Thames TV, 1992 (10 per cent)/Whitaker's Almanack

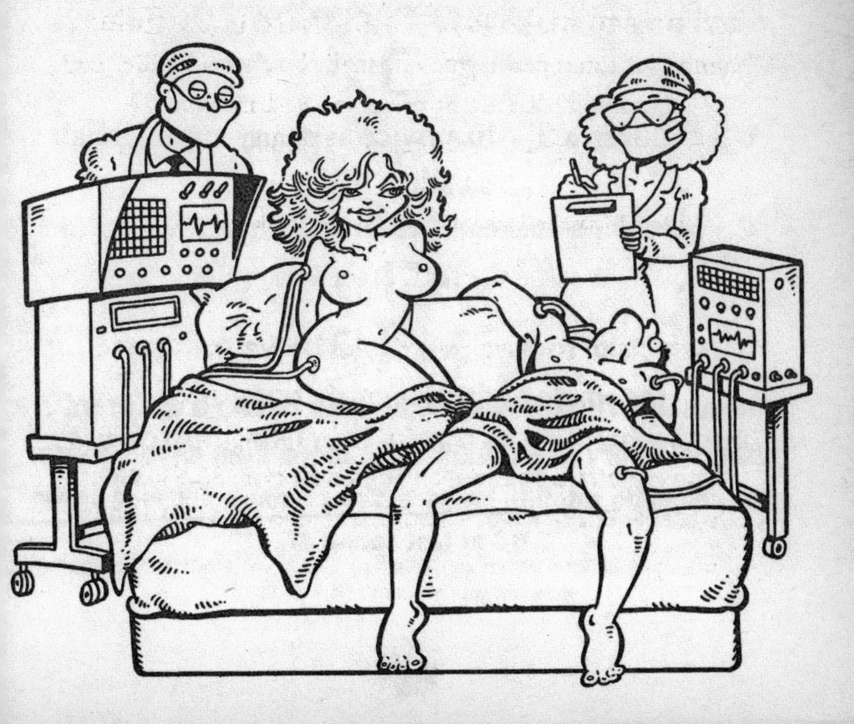

Recreational THERAPY

Americans have three times as many TV sets as Italians and 100 times as many as Nigerians have.

TVs per 1,000 Italians: 255. Per 1,000 Americans: 813. Per 1,000 Nigerians: 8.8.

OECD/Euromonitor: International Marketing Data and Statistics

US children's TV has twice as many commercials as adult TV.

Commercials per hour on US children's TV programming: 16.

M. Seiden, Access to the American Mind (USA)

Satellite TV viewers will be able to zap a different channel every five minutes for more than seven hours.

Non-domestic satellite broadcasting channels licensed by the ITC at last count: 87.

Hansard, vol. 248, no. 154, col. 1185

For every £1 it spends promoting the arts, Her Majesty's UK government spends 130 times as much buying supplies for war.

Annual procurement, research and development budget of the Ministry of Defence: £12 billion.

Arts Council grant-in-aid: £91.8 million.

UK Defence Budget, 1993/Hansard, vol. 234, no. 22, col. 765

The British book business is effectively a monopoly: England and Scotland's single biggest bookshop chains outsell all the others put together by nearly seven-to-one.

Sales of W.H.Smith (including Waterstones) and Menzies bookshops in the latest year: £2.55 billion.

Sales of all the other main bookshop chains put together: £379 million.

The Bookseller, no. 1993/24

A reader could buy a different book on royalty every Saturday for well over two years.

Books on royalty in print: 120.

Book Data Ltd/The Guardian

A cable subscription is four times more expensive than the TV licence fee, and a satellite subscription three times more.

Monthly Videotron cable TV subscription charge in April 1990: £10.94. In November 1994: £30.96. 30 Sky Channels: £22.99. Monthly TV licence fee rate: £7.

Torin Douglas, Marketing Week/Granada/Sky TV

A Briton could browse through a different newspaper every day for 274 years.

Chlorine per tonne of product released by paper recycling mills: 46gm. From virgin fibre mill: 1,900gm. From virgin fibre pulp (newspaper) mills: 4,900gm.

Writers' and Artists' Yearbook 1995/
Daniel Press, University of California Santa Cruz, New Scientist, no. 1944

Nearly a quarter of the American TV audience consists of children aged between two and 11.

M. Seiden, Access to the American Mind (USA)

71 out of 72 commercials on American TV are about spending.

Advertising Age (USA)

Warner Bros film studio moguls bought 700 screenplays they never made, or about 60 years of feature film production.

Variety

TV offers 53 hours of illusion for each hour of life.

Hours of programmes weekly in multichannel UK homes: 9,000.

Real-time hours in a week: 168.

British Audience Research Board/Continental Research Star Report, Marketing Week

To decide on Britain and the Commonwealth's best novel, a Booker Prize judge would need more than 15 years to read all the novels published in a year.

Novels per day read by 1994 Booker prize judges: 1.4 (130 books in 90 days, discounting 2x24-hour days/wk for work).

Novels published per year: 8,000.

Book titles expected in print by the end of 1994: 680,000.

Colman Getty Ltd/The Bookseller

Britons watch 26,000 years of TV per night.

British Audience Research Board

It would take a typical stage play 118 years to reach one *Coronation Street* audience.

Average 1993 attendance at a live modern drama production: 381.

Measured TV audience of Coronation Street on 31 August 1994: 16.35 million. (7 perfs/wk)

Society of London Theatre, Independent London/Broadcast

British cable TV operators want to devote nearly half their 200 new channels to – guess what? – mass-market advertising.

Rolling mass-audience menus proposed for 96 channels: 14.

Marketing Week, citing SBC CableComms

American non-readers can purchase Margaret Mitchell's sprawling epic love story *Gone With The Wind* on no fewer than 30 cassette tapes - a stack one-and-a-half feet high.

The Bookseller

40 per cent (39) of French cinema movies made in 1993 were by young first-time directors.

Variety

Rock 'n roll enters Iranian homes at a rate of 50 TV sets a working hour.

Estimated satellite dishes being installed daily in Iran: 400. Homes reached by MTV Europe's rock videos: 65 million.

Variety, citing Salam, Teheran

Women earn less than half what men earn in Hollywood acting parts.

A typical year's US female actor's earnings on film and TV: $296 million. Male actor's: $644 million.

Empire magazine

American viewers spend 3.5 million years watching TV commercials per year – the world audience when it reaches US levels will spend 77 million years. (30.6bn hours in US; today's population)

Earth Island Journal (USA)

Britain's BBC-TV could have screened a new 60-minute contemporary drama every week for over three years on the losses of one Hollywood movie.

New Yorker magazine/BBC-TV (Last Action Hero had lost $124m when taken out of US distribution; BBC drama £500,000/hr)

UK mainstream television, with no spiritual content, is two thousand times more accessible than the state religion.

British population per Anglican church: 3,235.

Population per TV set: 1.57.

The Church Commissioners/Office of Population Census and Surveys/ British Audience Research Board

Kids spend 70 times as much on computer games as rock guitars.

Acoustic guitar annual sales: £10 million.

Computer games: £700 million.

Music Industries Association/Independent on Sunday

About 108,000 average lifetimes could pass during a year's British TV viewing.

Average 24-hour days a year a Briton spends watching TV: 54.

Hours in a 75-year lifetime: 657,000.

British Film Institute Film and TV Handbook, 1994

TV offers 53 hours of illusion for each hour of life.

Hours of programmes available weekly in multichannel UK homes: 9,000. Real-time hours in a week: 168.

BARB/Continental Research Star Report, Marketing Week

It's happened: TV viewers spend more on buying tickets to stay home for transmitted films than going out to see them together at the cinema.

UK cinema box office take in 1993: $534 million.

Pay-TV take: $622.5

Variety

An average Briton born today can expect, in his or her lifetime, to watch TV for 11 solid years before dying.

BFI Film & TV Handbook 1994

It would take a typical London stage-play 118 years to reach the audience of one TV soap programme.

Average 1993 attendance at a live modern drama production: 381.

Measured 31 August TV audience of *Coronation Street*: 16.35 million.

Society of London Theatre (7 perfs/wk)/Broadcast (1994)

Children spend 12 times longer watching television in the evenings than doing school homework and 40 per cent longer watching TV than teachers year-round.

Hours' viewing per year: 1,391.

Hours of teacher viewing per year: 955.

David Blunkett MP. BFI Handbook citing AGB-BARB 26:44 hrs/wk (191 schooldays @ 5 hrs per diem)

CAR Mageddon

More than four world supertanker fleets of water are polluted during the manufacture of the 13.5 million new cars sold each year in Western Europe.

(1992 est. 405m tonnes)

DRI research

Population increase alone promises to add to UK traffic a queue of cars at least 128 miles long.

UK population increase per day predicted: 487.

People per car now: 2.6. Annual cars added to fleet: 68,000.

HMSO, Sustainable Development, the UK Strategy, 1994/Whitaker's Almanack 1994/RM (car=10ft)

A cyclist is killed by Shanghai drivers almost every day.

Shanghai cyclists killed each year: 350.

National Geographic, vol. 185, no. 3

More motor vehicles have been added to the UK fleet since Mrs Thatcher was elected Prime Minister than were possessed by the whole country in 1955.

Increase in UK vehicle fleet since Mrs Thatcher elected Prime Minister: 6.5 million. UK vehicle fleet in 1955: 6.45 million.

Whitaker's Almanack 1995/DVLC Swansea

Motor vehicles existing in the world would form a six-lane traffic jam to the Moon, or a three-lane traffic jam there and back. (645m @ 3.5 metre/vehicle)

Society of Motor Vehicle Manufacturers

More than twice as many buses are ordered off the road for faulty brakes as for diesel smoke emission.

Brake fault prohibitions 1992-93: 620.
Diesel smoke emission prohibitions: 259.

Ministry of Transport, Hansard, vol. 242, no. 94, col. 391

About 10,000 Britons a year are killed by fine particles from urban car exhausts.

New Scientist, 10 March 1994 (PM10 particles)

The channel tunnel will reduce freight time to southern Europe by only seven minutes an hour.

Time taken for a rail freight wagon to travel via ferry from Manchester to Avignon: 36 hours. By channel tunnel: 32 hours.

Hansard, vol. 240, no. 80(2), col. 1035

Every time one jar of strawberry yogurt is delivered to a supermarket in southern Germany, a 34-tonne lorry moves roughly 9.2 metres.

Kilometres of lorry freight required to load and deliver one truckful of 150-gm strawberry yogurts: 3,500.

Wuppertal Institute for Climate, Energy and Environment/Panoscope 39

For every two heavy lorries grinding through German neighbourhoods, there are three in Britain.

Percentage of Britain's freight going by road: 89. Of Germany's: 57.

Hansard, vol. 240, no. 80(2), col. 1035

By the year 2005, Americans will be wasting almost 8,000 centuries a year sitting in stopped traffic.

(7bn hours)

P. Hawken, The Ecology of Commerce, London, 1993

A child pedestrian is 151 times more likely to be killed or injured by a motor vehicle than an adult is to catch Aids.

Child pedestrians killed or injured by drivers in 1992: 1 in 264.

Britons catching Aids: 1 in 40,000.

Department of Transport (44,186 in 1992)/Whitaker's Almanack 1994 (children 11.7m); WHO/Department of Health (1992 rate 2.5 per 100K)

On a given day only one car in 13,000 gets stolen.

Average daily car thefts in 1992-3: 1,683.

Private and light goods vehicles registered in UK: 22,344,000.

Home Office (Hansard, vol. 235, no. 25, col. 272)/Whitaker's Almanack 1994

One-in-five buses are defective.

Passenger carrying vehicles officially inspected 1992–3: 39,065.

Found defective: 7,463.

Department of Transport, Hansard, vol. 236,no. 36, col. 388

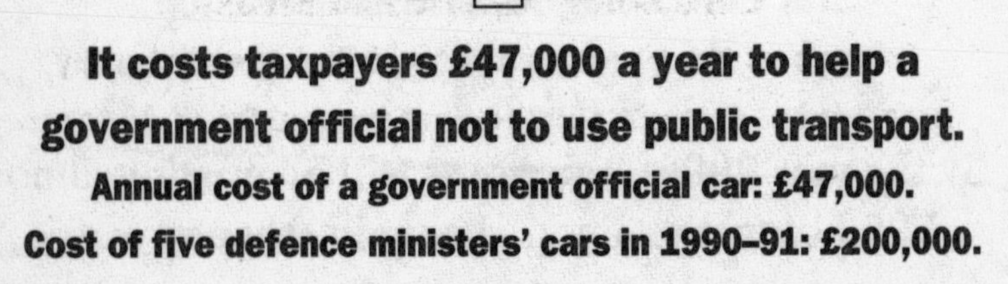

It costs taxpayers £47,000 a year to help a government official not to use public transport.

Annual cost of a government official car: £47,000.

Cost of five defence ministers' cars in 1990–91: £200,000.

Ministry of Defence, Hansard, vol. 235, no. 25, col. 174

For the cost of building London's M25 orbital motorway, 66 major Hollywood motion pictures could have been British-made.

Cost of building the M25 1972-86: £1 billion.

Current underway costs: £263.8 million.

Average cost of a Hollywood motion picture: £19.2 million.

Ministry of Transport, Hansard, vol. 238, no. 59, col. 698/British Film Institute Handbook, 1994

Japanese motor roads could pave the EC state of Luxembourg four times.

Square kilometres of the world taken up by Japanese roads: 11,500.

By the state of Luxembourg: 2,586.

'Japan 1994, An International Comparison', Keizai Koho Center, Tokyo, Japan/Hutchinson Pocket Guide to Countries of the World

Whitehall is preparing nearly 1,000 bridges for Euro semi-trailer truck invasion.

Bridges on the trunk road network being structurally assessed or strengthened to bear the weight of 40-tonne lorries: 972.

Ministry of Transport Highways Agency targets, Hansard, vol. 242, no. 94, col. 386

In England it is 14 per cent cheaper to license someone to experiment on animals than a car.

Personal licence under the Animals (Scientific Procedures) Act 1986: £108. Motor vehicle excise tax: £125.

Hansard, vol. 235, no. 26, col. 336/Driver & Vehicle Licensing Centre

In the last five years, British embassies abroad have spent the price of eleven bicycles a day purchasing motor vehicles. (£21m; bike £200)

Foreign and Commonwealth Office, Hansard, vol. 263, no. 133, col. 326

Five-and-a-half days and nights of the mighty Niagara Falls would be needed to supply the water required to make a year's motor vehicles.

Cubic metres of water a year polluted by manufacture of 2.3 million Fiat group vehicles: 162.5 million. Flowed by Niagara per second: 5,830. Annual world vehicle production: 43.78 million.

Fiat Environmental Report 1992/R. Ash, The Top Ten of Everything London, 1995

A different European motor vehicle could drive past you once every second round the clock for nearly nine years, and then the extra vehicles expected to be added in the meantime would take another nearly seven years to pass.

(281m non-2-wheel vehicles growing at 8 per cent; includes former USSR)

Euromonitor European Marketing Data and Statistics, 1994

Roads appear to be getting safer because vehicles force pedestrians off them.

Percentage of 7–8 year-olds going to school on their own in 1971: 80. In 1991: 9. Proportion of child pedestrians killed or injured by drivers in 1992: 1 in 264.

Alarm UK, 13 Stockwell Rd SW9 9AU/Department of Transport (44,186 in 1992)/Whitaker's Almanack, 1994 (children 11.7m)

The British travel less by rail and more by global-warming road than any other country outside North America, and 68 times more is spent advertising cars than trains in national newspapers.

Average daily motoring propaganda expenditure in UK national newspapers: £491,000. Rail propaganda: £7,202.

Worldwatch Institute, cited in Geographical vol 66, no. 6/ Register-MEAL (£179.4m p.a. on cars, £2.6m on rail, not counting colour supplements)

A completely catalysed car and van fleet could still pack 42 years of untreated tailpipe pollution into a day (and catalysers do not prevent global warming).

Minutes (approximately) taken by car exhaust catalyser to reach 300C operating temperature: 1.

Cars and vans in Britain: 22,344,000.

Society of Motor Manufacturers & Traders/DTI/Whitaker's Almanack 1994

By 2000, Thai drivers could be outbuying the British on new cars. New cars sold in Thailand in 1993: 456,000. In Britain: 1,778,000.

Thai sales in 2000 at current 30 per cent annual increase: 2,201,000.

Paris Match/Society of Automobile Manufacturers and Traders

Far from falling, child fares on London's public transport are set to have doubled within the span of one childhood.

Real percentage increase in London Transport fares since 1985: 32.7. In child fares: 69. Percentage of UK peak-hour car trips which convey children to school: 20.

Department of Transport, Hansard, vol. 243, no. 103, col. 276/ National Travel Survey

The public cost of traffic accidents on one short stretch of trunk road averages over £23,000 a day.

Cost of traffic accidents on the A64 Leeds-Scarborough over the last five years: £42.8 million.

Hansard, vol. 243, no. 102, col. 242

The Highways Agency was planning for motor traffic to triple within a decade on a rural Sussex trunk road.

Vehicles per day on the A27 from Lewes to Beddingham in 1993: 14,500. Median official forecast for 2003: 43,900. (low forecast 39,500, high 48,300)

Hansard, vol. 243, no. 102, col. 245

Thirty-eight times more is spent selling motoring to American TV viewers than civic culture.

Amount spent advertising automotive products on US television each day: $5.11 million. On religion, politics and unions: $134,000.

Motoring propaganda's percentage increase 1993–94: 27.

Variety

If you divide your mileage driven by the time you spend working to buy, driving, repairing, cleaning and otherwise attending to your car, you actually motor at an average speed slower than a horse.

Hours per year spent involved with a global-warming car by the average driver: 1,600.

Average m.p.h. driving speed, fully accounted for: 5.

Paul Hawken, The Ecology of Commerce, London 1993, citing Ivan Illich, Energy & Equity, London 1974

For every British car bought by South Koreans, British drivers buy 238 South Korean ones.

Cars imported to UK from South Korea since 1987: 74,431. Exported to South Korea: 313.

Hansard vol. 246, no. 135, col. 708

More than one in 10 people found guilty in court are offending drivers.

English and Welsh 1992 convictions for summary motoring offences in all courts: 6,146.

For indictable and summary non-motoring offences: 51,842.

Hansard, vol. 244, no. 112 ,col. 264

Drivers cause nearly as many serious injuries to non-drivers as they do to themselves.

Pedestrians, pedal and motor cyclists seriously injured on roads in 1991: 25,190.

All other road users injured on roads in 1991: 26,415.

David Pearce, Measuring Sustainable Development, London 1994

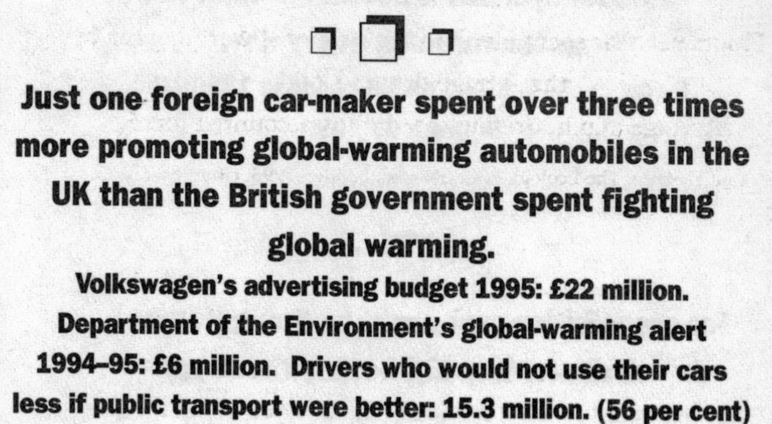

Just one foreign car-maker spent over three times more promoting global-warming automobiles in the UK than the British government spent fighting global warming.

Volkswagen's advertising budget 1995: £22 million. Department of the Environment's global-warming alert 1994–95: £6 million. Drivers who would not use their cars less if public transport were better: 15.3 million. (56 per cent)

Department of the Environment: 'Wasting Energy Costs The Earth', Campaign/ MORI/LexServices plc

In Los Angeles, 12 million people drive 8 million cars over 100 million vehicle-miles a day using half as much fuel as the entire former Soviet Union.

Tomorrow magazine (USA)

North America's cars guzzle an Olympic swimming pool of fuel every three minutes.
(plus 10 per cent for Canada; 150K US gallons/min)

Motor Vehicle Manufacturers' Association of the US

75 pedal cyclists are killed or injured by motor vehicles every day.
Pedal cyclists killed on UK roads in 1990: 256.
Injured: 27,108.

Whitaker's Almanack

Fewer than two minutes separate each British road accident injury. (336K in 1990)

Whitaker's Almanack

If there were only one British driver, and that driver drove all the miles driven by British cars in a year, she would go round the world 12 million times.

(499,000m km)

UK Department of Transport

Cars for Minnesota's Mall of America shopping car park could queue 36 miles. (12,750 spaces @ 4.5m)

Focus magazine

Turn on all the lights in every room in an average house, then two electric rings, the fridge, two TVs, a computer, and the washing machine, then do the same in another 20,000 homes–Toyota's car-making plant at Burnaston, England, could power the lot.

Wattage of Toyota's Burnaston car plant: 40 million.

Powergen advertisement

80 per cent of British drivers say they would find it very difficult to adjust their lifestyle to being without a global-warming car.

MORI

Cars in use throughout the world would stack to the moon–and beyond. (So would commercial vehicles: 147m of them @ 3m high.)

World car fleet: 478 million.

Median car-body height in feet: 4.5.

Average miles distance of Moon from Earth: 381,000.

Society of Motor Manufacturers & Traders

When the Chinese catch up with British car ownership, their little four-wheeled chunks of oil refinery will be capable of jamming up the whole of a six-lane highway stretching round the world six times.

Cars the Chinese would own if they were British: 405 million.

MORI/Whitaker's Almanack, 1995/
Hutchinson Guide to the World, London 1994

Five semi-trailer trucks would be required to carry UK vehicles' daily emissions of a cancer-causing toxin known to have no safe level of lifetime-exposure to human cells.

Tonnes of benzine evaporated or carburated from non-diesel vehicles in a year: 42,600. Percentage of atmospheric benzene which stems from cars: 78. UK retail fuel stations emitting evaporated benzine: 19,000.

Department of the Environment: Expert Panel on Air Quality Standards (1991)/
Euromonitor: European Marketing Data and Statistics

Police cars are involved in 54 accidents a day.

Home Office, Hansard, vol. 260, no. 109

By this time next year, cars passing through the main street of Newbury, England, will have spewed into the town centre at least 0.37 tonnes of lead, 4,719 tonnes of carbon dioxide, 1,911 tonnes of carbon monoxide, 683 tonnes of hydrocarbons and nitrogen oxides and 13 tonnes of sulphur dioxide, burning some 456,000 gallons of non-renewable fuel, or enough to circle the world 365 times.

Number of vehicles per day passing through Newbury on the A34 in 1988: 40,000.

In 1995: 50,000. Predicted in 2010: 65,000-78,000.

Secretary of State for Transport, Hansard, vol. 263, no. 133 (not counting commercial traffic, based on: EC 9359, all standard cars only, distance 1km, 78 per cent non-CAT, 20 mpg, 38 per cent leaded fuel @ 0.0107 gm/km; also D. Gordon, Steering a New Course, 1991, USA Union of Concerned Scientists, whence SO2 @ 0.14 gm/mi & CO2 @ 1.12 lb/mi)

Even after the introduction of catalysers and unleaded fuel, Britain's lead-polluting cars and vans could still queue from London to Chile and back. (38 per cent or 7.74m @ 10ft long)

MORI/Lex Services

On a given day, thieves steal only one car in 13,000, but nearly half of all drivers illegally speed on motorways and nearly three-quarters speed in built-up areas.

Average daily car thefts in Wales and England during 1992–3: 1,683. Private and light goods vehicles: 22,344,000. Percentage of cars exceeding the 70 mph speed limit by 10 mph: 48. Exceeding 30 mph urban speed limit: 69.

Home Office, Hansard, vol. 235, no. 25, col. 272/
Whitaker's Almanack/Local Transport Today, no. 162

The industrialized world reeled when the oil sheikhs suddenly boosted the price of oil by 70 per cent on 17 October 1973, but drivers went on to notch up twice the regular mileage they did before that.

Miles driven by average Briton in 1970: 2,000.
Miles driven by average Briton in 1989: 4,000.

OECD

A UK pedestrian is injured by motor vehicles every 34 seconds. (60,000/yr)

Whitaker's Almanack

In the space of five years, South Korea went from producing 30 per cent fewer motor vehicles than Britain to producing 11 per cent more.

Increase in South Korean motor vehicle production 1987–92: 980,000/1,730,000.

In British production: 1,390,000/1,540,000.

Hansard, vol. 235, no. 26, col. 307

Britain's Prime Minister requires £470,000-worth of car transport a year – including his Deputy, that's £2,000-worth a day.

Cost of Deputy Prime Minister's car service in one year: £230,000.

Hansard, vol. 240, no. 79, col. 790 (1992-93)/Press Association

The UK Department of Transport is entirely controlled by men.

Grade 6 males running the department: 21. Females: 0.

Female Department of Transport typists: 514. Male: 2.

Department of Transport, Hansard, vol. 247, no. 137, col. 70

Over 5,000 new climate-altering motor vehicles are produced every minute.

World total vehicle production in 1952: 8,320,091.

World total vehicle production in 1990: 44,165,033.

Automotive News, USA

The 1,200-mile cycle road network proposed for London would cost the same as 400 yards of the Jubilee Line underground rail extension.

Mayer Hillman/Policy Studies Institute

92 per cent overall of drivers driving recklessly, causing death or bodily harm, driving after alcohol or drugs, breaking speed limits, causing accidents, neglecting signs, directions or pedestrian rights, or driving carelessly are male.

Home Office Statistical Bulletin (1991)/The Pedestrian Association, Walk, Spring 1995

A keen driver could have test-driven a different 1994 car model every Saturday for 14 years.

Varieties of car on sale in Britain: 750.

Top Gear, BBC2-TV

Tyres scrapped in the USA in a year could form 10 stacks the size of the US Pentagon; those that get recycled could barely fill three of its five storeys.

US Environmental Protection Agency study on current and potential used tire markets, 1992/Quid, Robert Laffont, Paris (242m tires, 7 per cent recycled, Pentagon floorspace 60.4 hectares)

Roadside verges in the UK represent a potential nature reserve the size of the county of Berkshire.

Estimated hectares of greenery beside UK roads: 207,000.

Geographical, April 1995

A total jam-up of every lane of every motorway in Britain could accommodate only one in four motor vehicles.

Feet of motorway lane: 62.4 million.

Feet of vehicles: 251 million. (vehicle 10ft)

Whitaker's Almanack 1995

The volume of petrol pumped to fill a car equals the volume of gas emitted from the tank.

J. Emsley, The Consumer's Good Chemical Guide, W.H. Freeman, 1995

NASA's unbuilt Alpha space station has cost $4.3 million per working day for 10 years.

States collaborating on the construction of the space station: 17. Cost since 1984: $11.2 billion.

Boeing US TV commercial/Flight International

❐ ❐ ❐

To design their new plane, Boeing engineers could have used a different computer terminal every working day for eight years.

Computer workstations used simultaneously to design the Boeing 777 airliner: 2,200.

Business Life/British Airways

A passenger on a jet aircraft uses more (untaxed) fuel than a person travelling alone in a car, and four times as much as a full carload.

High estimate of miles per gallon of an airline passenger: 28. (6.6–10 l/100km)

Robert Egli/Lufthansa

The amount of tax-free fuel a typical uncatalysed Boeing 747 jumbo-jet carries could drive a catalysed family car round the world 60 times.

(Litres fuel capacity of a Boeing 747-N732: 178,709.)

Noisy night flights between 11pm and 7am at London's Heathrow Airport have increased by 50 per cent since 1988, and almost one car trip per second is made to the airport by passengers.

Average number of airliners per minute taking off from LHR: 1.1. (19.6m trips; 17-hr day)

Heathrow Association for the Control of Aircraft Noise, TW9 3DE/BAA

If it were a NASA Orbiter shuttle, spaceship Earth would be grounded.

Tonnes of tank fuel per Shuttle passenger: 87.5.

Tonnes of fuel left per Earth passenger: 25.

Quid 1995, Paris, Robert Laffont (700-tonne fuel tank)/BP World Oil Review, 1995 (Annual world tonnes of oil consumption: 3,132 million Tonnes of world oil reserves: 137 billion. Passengers on Earth: 5.5 billion)

Market-forces wreck planets: the price of non-renewable crude petroleum oils and crude oils obtained from bituminous minerals has dropped by one-fifth since 1990.

(1990 unit price: 100. In 1994: 80.6)

Central Statistical Office, Annual Abstract of Statistics 1995

Airlines for the rich pay at least four times less for fuel than buslines for the poor.

Approximate commercial cost of an undutied litre of jetliner kerosene: UK 12p.

Of a litre of bus DERV, including UK 28p duty: UK 50p.

Robert Egli, Office for Chemistry of the Atmosphere/Shell UK

Leaving British aviation fuel untaxed amounts to an annual public subsidy of £2.5 billion for the jet-set and their uncatalysed airliners.

Duty on a litre of bus DERV: 28p. On a litre of aviation turbine fuel: 0p. Litres of jet fuel sold in 1994: 9.09 billion.

UK Petroleum Industry Association/Shell UK.

Over half the 5,592 non-Soviet jet and turboprop civil airliners that were in service in 1968 are still being flown, wasting fuel and polluting the heavens.

Flight International

NASA is spending over half a million pounds a day ($910,000) developing a new range of uncatalysed supersonic airliners to burn toxic fuel close to the Earth's protective ozone layer.

NASA's 1995 working-day expenditure on a Concorde successor: £569,000 ($910,000).

The Engineer

It takes up to 2.2 litres of kerosene to air-freight one pound of fruit or vegetables across the world.

Robert Egli, citing Lufthansa (communication with author)

Imagine a 15,000-mile queue of road tankers spilling toxic gas across the fragile upper atmosphere round the northern hemisphere: that's a year's nitrogen oxides spewed out by airliner engines – which can't be fitted with catalysers: and they want to double air traffic!

Tonnes of ozone-depleting nitrogen oxides emitted in the upper atmosphere by jetliners each year: 3.5 million.
Number of times longer NOx pollutes the upper atmosphere than the lower: 100.

Robert Egli, Office for Chemistry of the Atmosphere, Schaffhausen, Switzerland

Airlines steal the sun for profit: on a typical blue-sky day in South-East England, up to 20 jet con-trails criss-cross the sky and spread into a haze.

Save Our Skies, PO Box 248 TW1 3DG.

The USA's subsidy for polluting air travel is 26 times bigger than Britain's.

UK taxpayer support for civil aerospace, direct and indirect in 1994–5: £23.6 million.

NASA civil aeronautics budget for 1994: $1.02 billion.

Department of Trade and Industry, House of Commons Official Report, vol. 251, no. 25

Crossover points on London's expanded M25 ring-road at Heathrow Airport will be wide enough for one taxiing jumbo jet to overtake another.

Number of lanes at crossover points: 26.

Yards of wingspan of Boeing 747 jumbo-jet: 65.

FLAME campaign, Runnymede (11ft per lane including hard shoulders)/ BA press office

Britain's whole air defence is based on one type of plane.

Number of active nuclear and sub-nuclear air strike planes available: 96. Number which are Tornado GR models: 96.

Ministry of Defence, Hansard, vol. 238, no. 60, col. 786

30 per cent more aircraft defend the UK now than at the height of the Cold War.

Number of aircraft defending UK air space in 1969: 60.
In 1994: 96.

Ministry of Defence, Hansard, vol. 238, no. 60, col. 786

Low-flying warplanes terrorize central Wales on average every three days.

Low-flying sorties flown since 1979: 1,662.
Tornado bombers crashed since 1990: 22.
Value: £250 million

Hansard, vol. 239, no. 71, col. 858/The Times 12.1.96

The average daily number of low-flying warplane sorties over peacetime Britain is 436.

Minimum RAF low-flying sorties over Britain made since 1979 inclusive: 2,390,000.
Low-level flights allowed in Germany: 0

Hansard, vol. 240, no. 79, col. 732/The Times 12.1.96

Satellites circling 20,000 kilometres above the Earth are used to position building piles to an accuracy of plus or minus 25 millimetres.

Building magazine

Lethal pieces of space junk in orbit could double in number within 14 years.

Larger items of space junk in orbit: 150,000.
Median number expected in 2003,
probable launch year of space station Alpha: 211,500.
(based on 2–5 per cent annual growth)

NASA communiqué, 27 June 1994

With air-conditioning halved, cases of tuberculosis infection in airliners are currently being investigated by the US Center for Disease Control.

Minutes between cabin air recycling on older airliners: 3.
On new airliners: 7.

Independent on Sunday

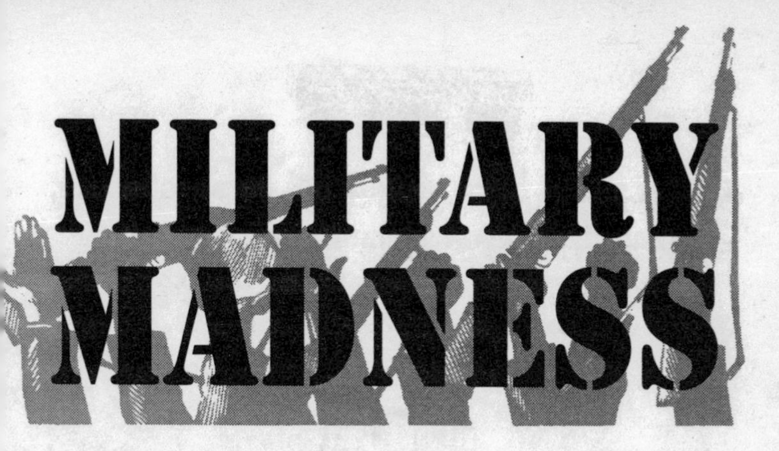

In 1989, more than one Swiss resident in three voted to have the ancient, 600,000-strong Swiss army completely abolished.

(Nov 1989 referendum 35.7 per cent)

NATO Review 6

War industry consumes almost half of all Britain's research and development funds.

John Pilger, New Statesman and Society, vol. 7, no. 322

❐ ❐ ❐

The UK's arms-sales office in Indonesia costs more than all the UK's elected legislators.

Working-day cost of Indonesian arms-sales office: £338,000.

Taxpayer support for MPs on an average working day: £212,000.

Ministry of Defence House of Commons Official Report, vol. 251, no. 25 (£90m/yr average 1991–93)/Speaker of the House of Commons (£57m/yr)

Britons spend twice as much as Swedes on war, and three times as much as Germans.

Annual war spending per Briton: US$1,450.

Per Swede: $700. Per German: $450.

IISS/Euromonitor

Since the fighter-bomber came into service, RAF pilots have crashed a Tornado while training on average once every six months.

Approximate cost of a Tornado: £20 million.

Percentage of the Tornados involved in low-level bombing of Iraq that crashed: 28.

House of Commons Official Report, vol. 257, no. 78, col. 397 (27 since 1981)/Ministry of Defence press office/Reuters (2 out of 7)

During the economic recession, Middle East states have been spending about £40 million per working day on war machinery.

Value of US arms sales in the Middle East 1990–93: $19 billion.

Of UK arms sales: $14 billion.

Percentage of females illiterate in Saudi Arabia: 69.

In Egypt: 71.

IDEX international arms exhibition, Abu Dhabi 1995/The Economist Book of Vital World Statistics

A forgotten landmine could explode somewhere every hour of every day for over 11,000 years.

Unexploded mines buried across the world: 100,000,000. (high estimate: 200m)

Crosslines/United Nations

British taxpayers support a bigger army now than when they faced Nazi Germany.

Regular Army strength in 1938: 114,000. In 1994: 123,028. Officers with their own chefs: 114.

Whitaker's Almanack 1939 and 1995/
Ministry of Defence House of Commons Official Report, vol. 251, no. 25

Hitler had destroyed more than 3.7 million German homes by May 1945.

Sean McKnight, VE Day in Photographs, Salamander 1995

Britons spend twice as much on war as the Japanese.

The UK defence budget (population: 57,000,000): $35,115,000,000. Japanese defence budget (population: 124,000,000): $35,900,000,000.

Ministry of Defence (1993–94)/Hansard, vol. 236, no. 40, col. 715

Peace? What Peace? between 1945 and 1976, 25 million people died in 133 wars.

Michel Tobias, Environmental Meditations, California, Freedom 1993

For every £1 it spends promoting the arts, UK government spends 130 times as much buying supplies for war.

Annual procurement, research and development budget of the Ministry of Defence: £12 billion. Arts Council grant-in-aid £91.8 million.

UK defence budget 1993/Hansard 234/22 col 765

47,565 people in Hampshire county, England, make a living from war.

Ministry of Defence, House of Commons Official Report, vol. 356, no. 69, col. 355

Providing most Ministry of Defence headquarters officials with an obsolete personal computer took 10 years and cost more than 50 times as much as a current machine.

Cost of secure 286-chip Ministry of Defence workstation: £38,000.
Typical retail cost of a 486-chip personal computer: £750.

Computer Weekly (Chots project)/PC World

Every working day, ferrying British war officials and their cargo between Britain and the USA costs £32,000. (average)

British Airways

To appraise hazardous wastes, a pollution team would have to inspect a different British government war-training area every working week for 43 years.

Weapons-firing or war-training areas operated by the UK nation-state: 2,266. (sites owned: 3,400, training/firing areas 2,266)

New Statesman & Society, no. 1950

The proportion of UK gross domestic product devoted to war is over one-third higher than the average of other NATO states. (36 per cent)

Nato Review, no. 2

It costs £48,000 a year to train an army cook.

Ministry of Defence (Army School of Catering, St Omer barracks, Aldershot)

North Korea may want an H-bomb – perhaps it's because the British government already has as many personnel dedicated to building nuclear warheads as North Korea has in its entire nuclear establishment.

Personnel employed building H-bomb warheads at Aldermaston: 5,000.

Estimated North Korean nuclear and technical personnel: 5,000.

New Scientist, no. 1,929/Song Ui-ho, The Korean/ Carnegie International Endowment for Peace/Vertic

The Ministry of Defence pays 12,400 bills a day – with your money. (3.3m p.a.)

Hansard, vol. 246, no. 135, col. 632

During two years of World War II battles the Soviet Union was losing an average of 876 army officers a day.

Red Army officers killed or missing in action June 1941–June 1943: 631,008. Members of Soviet forces killed in WW2: 8 million.

J. Erickson and D. Dilks: Barbarossa, the Axis and the Allies, London, 1994

The workforce of Britain's Ministry of Defence matches the biggest on the Stock Exchange.

Industrial workforce of the Ministry of Defence: 52,200. Of SmithKline Beecham PLC, health and household goods: 52,700.

Central Statistical Office, Annual Abstract of Statistics, 1995/The Times 1000, 1995

The war service is a bigger civilian employer than the rail service.

Employees of British Rail: 138,000.
Of the UK Ministry of Defence: 142,300.

Central Statistical Office, Annual Abstract of Statistics, 1995/The Times, 1000, 1995

Britain has a warship for every 20 of its merchant vessels.

UK warships: 97. UK merchant vessels: 1,998.

Ministry of Defence/Eurostat, Basic Statistics of the Community, Edition 30

A Briton spends 3.5 times more than a Spaniard on war.

War-related US dollars of gross domestic product spent annually by an average Briton: 301. By a Spaniard: 86.

Nato Review, no. 2

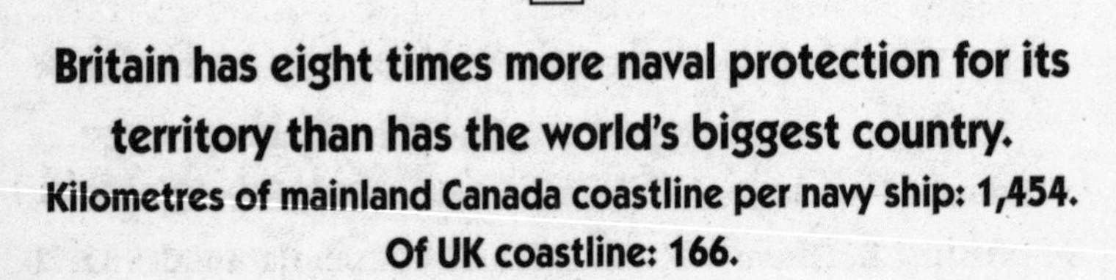

Britain has eight times more naval protection for its territory than has the world's biggest country.

Kilometres of mainland Canada coastline per navy ship: 1,454. Of UK coastline: 166.

Ministry of Defence (90 ships/15K km)/Canadian High Commission (49 ships/72K km)

The government's research workshops subsidize war to the armed services of 15 per cent of the political world.

States publicly-funded research is sold to: 24. UN states: 166.

Ministry of Defence, Hansard, vol. 263, no. 133, col. 270

Battle tanks ordered by the UK in 1994: 285. Battle tanks engaged in Germany's attack on Moscow in October 1941: 20,000.

Secretary of State for Defence 18 July 1994/Chronicle of the 20th Century, London 1988

The RAF spends nearly five times more on housing its dignitaries than the Church does.

The Church supports 45 official residences of diocesan bishops and archbishops and 69 houses of suffragan bishops, costing up to £3 million a year: average £26,300. The armed services maintains 77 official service residences costing £10.03 million a year: average £130,260.

Departments of National Heritage and Defence, Hansard, vol. 247, no. 137, cols 13 & 64

In the London blitz (September 1940–May 1941) it took a ton of bombs to kill three-quarters of a Londoner; in the Gulf War, it took three tons of 'precision-guided munitions' to kill an Iraqi child.

Winston S. Churchill, Chronicle of the 20th Century, 1988, London/Allied Coalition high command, 9 February 1991, BBC News and Current Affairs (1.08m t @ 20k t per day)/Harvard Medical Team 1991 (350,000 child typhoid deaths from Coalition's destruction of civil power supplies)

With one full-scale nuclear attack by a single Trident submarine, Britain's Royal Navy could cause 10 million civilian deaths, or 74 Dresdens.

Cities within 7,200 km strikable by a Royal Navy Trident submarine: 192. High estimate of fatalities in 14 February, 1945 fire-bombing of Dresden, Germany: 135,000.

Author estimate on basis of Nagasaki (50,000 fatalities per warhead)/Focus, August 1994/Hutchinson Pocket 20th Century World History, London, 1994

Public backing for war actually increases by 3 per cent every Christmas.

Percentage of DTI export credit which went to arms sales in 1980–81: 6.5. In 1993–4: 48.

World Development Movement, cited in New Statesman and Society (Export Credit Guarantee)

Before the civil-war ceasefire, the Northern Ireland Office and the emergency armed forces spent an estimated £52,000 ($83,000) a working day on press and public relations. (£14m in 1989)

D. Miller, Don't Mention The War: Northern Ireland Propaganda and the Media, Pluto 1994

A queue of 2,521 semi-trailer trucks stretching 24 miles would have been required to deliver enough TNT to match the power of a 1969 Soviet H-bomb test.

Hiroshima blasts equated by the Russian test: 2,900.

Geographical, vol. 66, no. 7

Just one complaint of racial harassment in the army and air force was substantiated in 1993.

Department of Employment, Hansard, vol. 235, no. 25, col. 265

New rooms for Royal Navy officers and ratings cost £40,000 each.

Cost of new 729-room residential mess opened at RN HMS Osprey, Portland in 1988: £29.8 million.

Hansard, vol. 247, no. 140, col. 391/RN Portland press office

The UK's aid contribution to Malaysia's Pergau Dam cost less than building the British state defence procurement headquarters.

Cost of the Defence Procurement Executive offices: £255.4 million. Britain's aid contribution to the building of the Pergau Dam: £234 million.

Ministry of Defence/Overseas Development Administration press office

The cost of the government's new arms-dealing headquarters could have built an Olympic sports stadium and staged in it an athletics event worth £65 million.

Cost of the Defence Procurement Executive offices: £255.4 million. Cost of Manchester's proposed stadium: £187 million.

Home Office, Hansard, vol. 235, no. 26, col. 339)/
Ministry of Defence/Building magazine

At least 21,000 personnel were physically close to British atmospheric A-bomb tests.

Hansard, vol. 244, no. 112, col. 231

Thirteen days separated the Royal Navy test-firing its H-bomb doomsday weapon, Trident II D5, and the French state testing a nuclear bomb in the Pacific.

Ministry of Defence (HMS Victorious, 24 July and 22 August 1995)/Reuters (5 September 1995)

The Cold War over, the British government still spends twice as much on war as on education.

Current estimated 1993–4 outturn for the Ministry of Defence: £23.4 billion. For the Department for Education: £9.8 billion. British jobs dependent on air travel or air war: 147,400.

Hansard, vol. 243, vol. 102, col. 234/Hansard, vol. 244, no. 112, col. 287

One recruit to an armed service recruiting office costs a staggering £4,296.

In 1993, 251 Ministry of Defence offices recruited 10,494 personnel at a cost of £45,090,000.

Hansard, vol. 242, no. 96, col. 550 (1993–94)

Over three-quarters of Britain's military sales are to régimes destroying both natural resources and indigenous peoples to pay for them.

Value of 1992 defence equipment exports to developing countries: £1,156 million. Percentage of total military exports: 77.

Hansard, vol. 244, no. 112, col. 318

Fielding an equipped member of the UK armed services costs nearly six times as much as fielding a German one.

Cost per capita of Britain's 646,500 regular and reserve forces by overall defence budget: $131,183.

Of West Germany's 1.35 million forces: $22,934.

Euromonitor, European Marketing Data and Statistics, 1994 (1992 figures)

In one year, US military personnel were converted to the civilian sector at a rate of 24,500 a working day, meaning today's USA world-wide armed forces could be disbanded in four months.

US armed forces in 1945: 8,266,373.

In 1946: 1,889,690. In 1993: 1,807,000.

The World Almanac and Book of Facts 1994, Funk and Wagnalls Corporation, NY USA

Heavy artillery shells used by British forces since 1985 have cost approximately £37,000 a day.

155mm shells type L15 fired per day on average: 30. Type M107: 67. Cost: £135 million.

Ministry of Defence, Hansard, vol. 242, no. 94, col. 395 and Hansard, vol. 241, no. 86, col. 501

An African dictator could visit a different accredited British war factory every working day for nearly four years.

UK war equipment manufacturers with 'quality system certification': 1,000.

Ministry of Defence, Hansard, vol. 241, no. 86, col. 506

The Health *Conspiracy*

Next time you think we've never been so healthy, remember the UK's National Health Service has to perform eight operations a minute round the clock.

General and acute NHS elective surgical operations carried out in the last quarter of 1993: 1,062,000.

Hansard, vol. 240, no. 80 (2) col. 1051

Year of the first popular article linking sunshine with cancer: 1941.

Dr Dean Black, 'Health & Wellness Report', Ladies' Home Journal, USA, Tapestry Press

Japanese medical researchers publish a scientific paper every minute of the working day. (109,700 p.a.)

Nature, no. 372, 1994

Bacterial resistance in Britons to penicillin is six times more likely than in 1989.

British Medical Jornal, vol. 6962, no. 309

Only one in 63 births occurs at home but, miraculously, a lucky baby is born at home every 50 minutes.

1993 Institutional births in England and Wales: 662,423. At home: 10,528.

Department of Health, House of Commons Official Report, vol. 251, no. 25 (Eng/Wales)

Hungary could provide every licensed premises in Greater London with 82 alcoholics.

Annual cirrhosis of the liver deaths among 10.5 million Hungarians: 4,080. Chronic liver disease and cirrhosis deaths among 57 million Britons: 3,571.

British Medical Journal, vol. 6977, no. 310 (10 per cent in 1993)/Whitaker's Almanack 1995/Central Statistical Office, Annual Abstract of Greater London Statistics, vol. 24

Nearly half of Asia's human population is infected with tuberculosis.

WHO, cited in Panos Aids Media Briefing

A patient could endure a different daily side effect of a £20.77 dose of Seroxat anti-depressant for 22 days. (Cost of Seroxat tablet: 69p)

SmithKline Beecham Phamaceuticals

❐ ❐ ❐

If everybody estimated to be HIV-positive could be persuaded to take AZT, its maker Glaxo-Wellcome's retail sales would increase by more than $20 billion a year.

People estimated to be HIV-positive: 17 million. Average cost of a year's treatment with zidovudine (AZT): $1,200. (AZT, viewed as a flop, has been industrially reaffirmed as a co-treatment for HIV/Aids)

Panos Aids Media Briefing

❐ ❐ ❐

107,000 Swiss people, including doctors, used their democracy to sign a petition demanding that possession and consumption of unlisted drugs was a personal matter underworld barons should not profit from and should be decriminalized – a remarkable one in every 62 people. (107,000 out of 6.62m)

British Medical Journal, no. 6965, vol. 309

Broke little communist Cuba is 75 per cent better supplied with doctors than Britain.

People per doctor in Cuba: 207. In Britain: 362.

Fidel Castro, ITV Network First (51,000)/General Medical Council (UK 160,000)

Half of all prescription items cost less than the prescription charge.

Prescription items dispensed in 1993: 445.4 million. Costing less than the prescription charge: 223 million.

Department of Health, House of Commons Official Report, vol. 251, no. 25

The cost of bad health is mounting by nearly a quarter every five years.

Percentage increase in the real-terms cost of the NHS since 1978–9: 69. Average health spending per person per year in the industrialized world: $1,250. In South Asia and sub-Saharan Africa: $5.

Department of Health, House of Commons Official Report, vol. 251, no. 25/Panos Aids Media Briefing

For every $1 spent by the British government on breast cancer research, the USA government spends $100.

Women's Environmental Network newsletter No.27

In the next three days, 10 semi-trailer truck-loads of aspirin tablets will be consumed worldwide.

(100bn/yr; tablet 300mg)

The Aspirin Bureau cited in PR Week, 24 March 1995

Cannabis is much less dangerous than common pain-killers.

People hospitalized for poisoning by paracetamol, acentanilide and phenacetin 1990–91: 30,479.

Department of Health, Hansard, vol. 242, no. 94, col. 370

The NHS could automate the rest of its medical practices with only 45 days worth of its office equipment budget.

Percentage of the 19,508 medical receptionists who do not possess a computer to hold practice records: 21. NHS office equipment expenditure in 1992–3: £36,573,000. Price of 386-model Vtech Computer including software package: £1,099.

Department of Health, Hansard, vol. 242, no. 94, col. 370 (1993 survey) and vol. 235, no. 25, col. 329/Vtech Computers advertisement/ Department of Health

Israel has nearly half as many doctors again as Britain.

Proportion of Israelis who are medical doctors: 1:400. Of Britons 1:581. Medical doctors immigrating to Israel per day over the last three years: 6.4.

British Medical Journal, vol. 308, no. 6938/British Medical Association inquiry desk (varies depending on practising or qualified)

It would take 12 sets of the *Encyclopedia Britannica* to hold the 'letters' of one person's genetic profile.

Letters in the DNA alphabet needed to make a human being: 300 billion.

Focus, The World In Perspective

French doctors could experiment on a different currently available orphaned human embryo every working day for the next 42 years.

Estimated 'supernumerary' human embryos in France: 11,000.

Nature, vol. 369, no. 6482

In Nigeria, up to one prostitute in five has Aids.
Cost of intercourse in a Nigerian brothel: $1–$2.50.
The World Health Organization's prediction of world Aids deaths by 2020: 121 million.

Panos Institute, WorldAIDS, no. 34

On their long journey into costly hospital treatment paid for by all, clients of the UK tobacco industry together consume about 670,000 tonnes of tobacco a year, or enough to load a nose-to-tail juggernaut jam from Birmingham to Penzance.
(semi-trailer truck 23t, 50ft: 275 miles)

Hansard, vol. 240, no. 78, col. 666

The market rations doctors: Italians have twice as many as Americans.
Physicians per 10,000 Italians: 42.4. Per 10,000 Americans: 21.4.
Number of times the earnings of an average doctor exceed the pay of a typical worker in the USA: 5.4. In Britain: 2.4.

'Japan 1994, An International Comparison'. Keizai Koho Center, Tokyo, Japan/Statistical Yearbook 1987, UN/Derek Bok, The Cost of Talent New York, Free Press, 1993

The National Health Service is nine times better value than commercial health insurance.

Annual cost of the NHS per Briton: £66.47.
Of B-scale BUPA cover for 34-year-old person: £580.92.

Department of Health, Hansard, vol. 236, no. 36/BUPA inquiry

Twelve times more for menstruation than for mercy.

Annual advertising budget of The Samaritans: £400,000. Launch advertising budget of new Lil-lets applicator tampon: £5 million.

Marketing Week

Britons only spend two-and-a-half times as much on the National Health Service as on the BBC.

Total NHS expenditure 1992-3: £3,789 million. Total BBC expenditure (excluding the World Service) 1992–3: £1,500m.

Department of Health, Hansard, vol. 236,no.36/BBC corporate press office

Women estimated to die each year from the complications of unsafe surgical abortion: 200,000.

Baroness Chalker/The Independent, 11 July 1994

More money in sickness than prevention: 210 more Scots went to hospital each day in 1992 than two years earlier.

Scottish admissions to hospital in 1990 (not counting transfers): 807,509. In 1992: 884,395. Number of times clinical waste produced annually in Greater London would fill Trafalgar Square to the height of Nelson's Column: 3.

Scottish Office, Hansard, vol. 236, no. 36, col. 315/British Medical Association/London Waste Regulation Authority (1987–8)

White men born during the baby boom are three times more likely to develop cancers unrelated to smoking as their grandfathers were; white women are 30 per cent more likely than their grandmothers to get such cancers.

Journal Of The American Medical Association

Public funding for UK medical research into Alzheimer's disease has been reduced by a fifth.

Expenditure in 1988–89: £5 million. Constant spending adjusted for 6 per cent inflation: £6.3 million. Actual expenditure: £4.9 million.

Hansard, vol. 240, no. 80(2), col. 1043

People have to keep dying of smoking: government tobacco revenues equal one-fifth the whole National Health Service bill.

Government 1993 revenues from tobacco products: £7,394,000,000.

Gross NHS expenditure 1992/93 £36,400,000,000.

HM Treasury, Hansard, vol. 236, no. 36, col. 352/Dept of Health press office

If UK women had babies at the same rate as Kenyan women, the isles' population would double to 115 million in 18 years.

Average number of children born to Kenyan woman completing her childbearing years: 8.1. To a UK woman: 1.8. Kenyans' annual percentage growth rate: 3.8. Official UK population growth prediction 1991-2001: 1,613,000.

The Economist Book of Vital World Statistics (1985-90)/
Census Reports, Whitaker's Almanack 1994

At its current rate of increase, the population of England and Wales by the year 3000 will be 213 million.

1992-93 net increase in Wales and England population : 162,000.

Geographical (to 51.44m)

If China's population ever matched its birth-sex ratio, there would be 74 million spare men, or 13 times the population of Hong Kong.

Male Chinese born per 100 females: 113.8. Male South Koreans born per 100 females: 113.6. (based on current population)

Private Decisions, Public Debate: Women, Reproduction and Population, Panos Institute, London

Four years of tobacco advertising would pay to control world population growth.

Annual advertising spend of major world tobacco companies: $4.6 billion. Cost of Cairo Agreement's world population stabilization programme to 2000: $17 billion.

British Medical Journal/Sex, Sin & Survival, Jonathon Porritt, C4TV

With the help of the UK Department of Health, which both promotes and regulates it, the medical industry got Britons to more than double their drug spending in a decade.

(£22.80 per Briton in 1982/£52.87 in 1992, prices adjusted for comparison)

UK Department of Health

Born in Britain, baby Jesus would have more chance of being fed by a factory than by the Madonna.

Milupa plc (55 per cent of UK babies on formula)

Britain's non-domestic coolers, freezers and fridges...many of them in hospitals... leak over 4,000 tonnes of CFCs a year, or the entire CFC bank every five years.

Department of the Environment, CFCs in UK Refrigeration

So-called poor Abkhasians age five times better than so-called rich Americans.
Percentage of the USA's over-65s considered fully functional: 18.
Percentage of Abkhasians over 90 judged mentally healthy and outgoing: 85.

D. Chopra, Ageless Body, Times Mind Crown Publishers Inc, 1993

All the fresh Siberian leopard skins left in the universe would not buy a new Mercedes convertible.

Median estimate of number of amur leopards left on the planet: 40. Sterling equivalent of price asked for amur leopard skin in a Vladivostock newspaper: £1,986. Cost of a Mercedes Benz SL600: £94,600.

National Geographic, vol. 185, no. 6/Mercedes Benz (UK) Ltd

A seal travelled 167,000 times its own length across ice and snow before freezing.

Kilometres from the shore of Antarctica where explorers found a frozen seal: 250. (seal length=1.5m)

Norwegian Polar Institute/New Scientist 1908

Britain's domestic cats are believed to have tormented and killed 20,000,000 birds.

World Watch magazine Jan–Feb 1994

A Harp seal's pelt is worth about nine times less than a Harp seal's penis.

Far-East street value of seal penis powdered to aphrodisiac: $US130. Of seal pelt: $US9–15.

Sea Shepherd Log, 1st quarter 1995

Norwegian whale-killers have treble vision.

Iceland's whale-killers estimate of Minke whale numbers in the North Atlantic: 28,000. Norway's: 89,000.

Sea Shepherd, 3107A Washington Bd, Marina Del Rey CA 90292

Today, humans will kill at least 2,700 super-intelligent porpoises and dolphins.

The typical brain-to-spinal cord ratio of a human: 50:1. Of an ape: 8:1. Of a bottlenose dolphin: 40:1.

Dolphins: Their Life and Survival, London 1994

Couples of royal eagles estimated left in France: 100.

Paris Match, no. 2372

The British perform vivisection on 80 per cent more dogs than the French.

Annual number of tests on dogs in British labs: 8,817.

Dogs used in French labs: 4,965.

Ministère de la Recherche (1993)/
Statistics of Scientific Procedures on Living Animals (1993), Home Office, 1995

Means of death of five zoo-bred California condors released into the wild:

Crashed into utility poles: 3. Electrocuted by power lines: 1.

Drank antifreeze in a parking lot: 1.

National Geographic, vol. 188, no. 2

For every tiger poached in India, there are roughly eight to 10 leopards killed.

Leopards in the state of Himachel Pradesh: 821.

Homo sapiens: 6.7 million.

Ratio of homo sapiens to leopards: 8,160:1.

New Scientist, no. 1990/India High Commission

The Indian sub-continent's tiger population is one-thirteenth what it was 60 years ago.

Estimated sub-continental population of tigers in the 1930s: 40,000. Today's population of tigers: 3,000.

Focus, The World In Perspective, June 1994

For every hour of the day and night, Americans scoff 10,000 lobsters.

In Context magazine (USA)

Italian men kill nearly a million songbirds a week for bite-size morsels.

'Protected' birds gunned down by Greeks each year: 700,000.
Songbirds killed by humans in Italy each year: 50,000,000.
Transiting birds shot each year for fun or food in Cyprus: 3,000,000.

Hellenic Society for the Protection of Nature/
National Audubon Society/World Watch, Jan–Feb 1994

The Americans are performing between three and 35 times as many laboratory experiments on live animals as the British.

Estimate-range of USA experiments on animals: 10 million–100 million. UK experiments in latest year: 2.8 million.

Les Krantz, America By The Numbers, New York 1993 (no official record kept)/Home Office, HMSO CM 2746 (1993)

Hunters or drivers killed nearly as many Florida black bears in the 1980s as are left on Earth.

Florida black bears killed by hunters 1980–91: 460.
Bears killed by automobile drivers: 234.
High estimate of bears surviving: fewer than 1,000.

Booth Gunter, Tampa Tribune 20 November 1991

A Javan rhinoceros is almost as rare as a painting by Vermeer.

Javan rhinoceros believed left alive: 60.

Dutch masters ascribed to Vermeer: less than 40.

Hutchinson Pocket Dictionary of the Environment, London, 1994/
Phaidon Encyclopedia of Art and Artists, London, 1978

China's impotent old men could wipe out wild tigers in eight years.

Tigers represented by China's four-month 1.5-ton tiger bone exports for aphrodisiacs June-Sept 1993: 200.

Low estimate of world's wild tigers: 4,600.

World Watch, vol. 7, no. 4/
Convention on International Trade in Endangered Species

North America's mighty Columbia River has lost over 80 per cent of its wild salmon since the New Deal.

Columbia river wild salmon in 1933: 16 million.

In 1993: 2.5 million.

Dams on the Columbia/Snake river system: more than 100.

Jeanne McDowell, Time 2 March 1993/
1994 Environmental Almanac, New York, 1993

The lifespan of a Kenyan elephant is worth $900,000 in tourist revenue.

Tourists visiting Africa in 1990: 9 million.

Predicted in 2000: 24 million.

Panos Institute, Media Briefing, no. 14

The largest existing mammal is 70 million times bigger than the smallest.

Grams weighed by the smallest shrew: 2.

Tonnes weighed by the largest whale: 140.

The Hutchinson Dictionary of Science, London, 1994

Canadian trappers maim and then kill as many as 250 wild foxes a day.

Wild fox pelts taken in Canada in one year: 91,414. (1987–88)

Canada Yearbook, 1992

For every human killed by a shark, 4.5 million sharks are killed by humans.

Observer Life, 1 August 1994

The English wiped out their wolves 800 years before the French.

Year deliberate extermination programme finally wiped out English wolves: 1290. Year last wolf seen in France: 1929. Cases of a healthy wolf eating a healthy human in the history of the USA: 0.

Focus magazine (citing Wolf Watch UK)/The Independent (citing Adirondack Wolf Project)

Less than half of the coastline of Japan's four main islands remains in a natural state. (46 per cent)

OECD/Nature, vol. 369, no. 6475

Japan increased her manufacturing output by nearly half in 14 years, and sacrificed at least one-seventh of her natural forests in doing so.

1979–1993 percentage output growth of Japan: 43. Of the UK: 5. Percentage decrease of Japan's natural forests due to development 1973–86: 14.

OECD/Nature, vol. 369, no. 6475/Hansard, vol. 244, no. 112, col. 319

Ten million people are evicted every year by development projects.

The World Bank/The Ecologist, vol. 24, no. 3

Nearly three-quarters of the Earth's surface is water and nearly a third of its land is desert.

Focus, August 1994 (71 per cent, including polar icecaps)/
Hutchinson Pocket Dictionary of the Environment, London,1994

Since World War II, 45 per cent of the UK's ancient semi-natural forest has been damaged or destroyed.

Percentage of forests in Wales & England which are semi-natural: 1.6. In Scotland: 1. In Western Europe: 1.5.

World Wildlife Fund/Geographical, vol. 66, no. 7

In India little more than one person in a million is giving serious thought to the future of one-sixth of humanity.

People in India seriously engaged in redesigning the future: 1,000.

Living wholly or primarily in the past: 790,000,000.

Satish Seth, Futures, vol. 19, no. 5, 1987, cited in A. Tough, Crucial Questions About the Future, London 1991

Nearly one-quarter of Britain's entire trade deficit is attributable to wood and plywood products.

Percentage of UK wood supplies imported: 85.

Geographical magazine

Killing a turkey a minute for British Christmas would take 100 working years.

Turkeys slaughtered for Christmas: 11 million.

Turkey Marketing Council

Enough wild mountain gorillas remain in existence for British zoos alone to have fewer than three each.

Mountain gorillas left in the world: 640. Licensed zoos and wildlife parks in Britain: 226. In Eastern Europe: 500.

Fauna and Flora Preservation Society/British Tourist Authority/Department of Environment, Hansard, vol. 247, no. 137, col. 38/State of the Ark, BBC2-TV, 21 July 1994

Unpolluted beluga whales can dive to a depth three times the height of London's NatWest Tower, and surface to breathe the air. (1,800 ft)

National Geographic, vol. 185, no. 6

The Indian sub-continent's tiger population is 13 times thinner than it was in the 1930s and that of humans three times greater.

Estimated sub-continental population of tigers around 1935: 40,000. Indians per square mile in 1930s: 211. Tigers today: 3,000. Humans per square mile: 672.

Focus, The World In Perspective, June 1994/Whitaker's Almanack 1939/The Hutchinson Guide To The World (India, Pakistan & Bangladesh)

The world's fishing fleets cost nearly twice as much as their catch.

Estimated worldwide expenditure on commercial fishing: $124,000,000,000.

Estimated value of the world fish catch: $70,000,000,000.

UN Food and Agriculture Organisation, cited in State of the World 1994, Worldwatch Institute, Earthscan

The mouth of a recently designed Icelandic trawling net is large enough to trap 12 jumbo-jets in piles of six simultaneously.

Peter Weber, 'Abandoned Seas: Reversing the Decline of the Oceans', Worldwatch Paper 116

The Black Sea has been given between 3,650 and 5,475 days to live.

Estimated cost of Black Sea sewage sources treatment: $1 billion.

Tonnes of Black Sea fish caught in 1986: 900,000. In 1992: 100,000.

Vladimir Dvoretsky, Panoscope, no. 38

Half the earth's surface is three kilometres or more below sea level.

Peter Weber, 'Abandoned Seas: Reversing the Decline of the Oceans', Worldwatch Paper 116 (Nov 1993)

Researchers found 476 items of manufactured rubbish per hour on an uninhabited Pitcairn Islands beach 5,000 kilometres from any big city in the Pacific.

New Scientist, vol. 1, no. 925

The global fish catch more than quadrupled from 20 million tonnes in 1950 to a peak of 86 million tonnes in 1989.

Estimated supertanker-loads of sea life of the wrong species or size that are caught, killed and thrown back into the sea per annum: 100.

Geographical, vol. 66, no. 6 (supertanker=100K t)

ENERGY

A gas-fired power station wastes over half (55 per cent) of its energy.

Percentage energy efficiency of a gas-fired power station: 45.

Department of Employment, Hansard, vol. 235, no. 25, col. 217

Making daily trips, a keen hydrologist would need 205 years to visit all the USA's dams.

Dams in the USA: 75,000.

'The Power, Promise and Turmoil of North America's Fresh Water', National Geographic, Washington DC, 1993

Although official estimates give British gas reserves just 26 years, domestic gas prices are falling.

Percentage real-terms reduction in gas bills since 1985: 31.

'Prospects For Coal: Conclusions of the Government's Coal Review', command paper 2235/Paying the Price, 1993 National Consumer Council

World oil consumption could empty the known reserves of Saudi Arabia in 11 years.

Euromonitor International & European Marketing Data & Statistics 1994 (3,247m t)/Allan M Findless, The Arab World, Routledge 1994 (35,000m t)

Far from conserving its non-renewable natural gas resources, Britain is accelerating production.

Millions of therms of gas produced in 1989: 477,500.
In 1993: 703,900.

Nature, vol. 373, no. 6514

Non-renewable global-warming fuel oil is cheaper now than it was in 1987.

Estimated value of oil extracted by Shell Oil Company from Ogoni tribal lands in Nigeria in 30 years: £200 billion.

Central Statistical Office Annual Abstract of Statistics, table 18.4/Earth First!

At US rates of ownership, the world's population in 2010 would have well over 2,000 million cookers, requiring 500 major power stations.

Author/Guinness Book of Answers, 9th Edition/Predicast Forecasts

Russia's oil pipelines leak enough energy every year to power one-third of humanity for a fortnight.

Barrels of ex-USSR oil & oil-products spilt annually: 28.5 million. Barrels consumed per day by China: 2.1 million. (5m t)

Prof Alexei Yablokov, Royal Institute of International Affairs

If every house in the UK had a solar panel supplementing its hot water system, at least 100 supertanker-loads of global-warming carbon dioxide emissions would be saved annually.

Minimum number of electrically lit households throughout the world: 747 million.

Centre for Alternative Technology, Machynlleth SY20 9AZ (12-hour day; 10m t)/ Euromonitor: World Marketing Data and Statistics, 1994 (latest years: early 1980s)

A 30-minute telephone call from London to Manchester uses 330 times less energy than the equivalent car journey: replacing one in 10 car trips with a phone call could conserve half the production of Britain's biggest oil refinery.

Amount spent on motor vehicles in the last five years by British embassies: £21 million.

BT and the Environment, 1994 (0.3 per cent)/BP Oil UK (10 per cent of 6.6bn gals petrol/yr; Milford Haven 3.5m gals/day)/FCO Hansard, vol. 263, no. 133, col. 326

By this time tomorrow, British car drivers will have burnt another 36 Olympic swimming poolfuls of their petrol reserves, and world drivers will have burnt 1,150 or enough to fill the Great Pyramid of Cheops.

RM (pool=500K gals)/BP Oil UK (UK 6.6 billion gals/yr; world 210bn)/Quid 1995

Domestic freezers sold every year in Britain would make 112 stacks as high as Mont Blanc.

1992 UK home freezer sales: 600,000.

Metres altitude of Mont Blanc: 4,807. (freezer height 90cm)

Euromonitor Consumer Europe 1993/Whitaker's Almanack 1994

A coal-fired power station wastes two-thirds of its energy.

Percentage efficiency of a coal-fired power station: 34.

Department of Employment, Hansard, vol. 235, no. 25 col. 217

The cost of air-conditioning in Houston, Texas is estimated to be equal to that of the GNP of 30 other countries.

Focus, The World In Perspective, August 1994

A Saudi Arabian uses three times less petroleum than a North American.

Tonnes of petroleum used annually per Saudi Arabian: 0.376.
Per North American: 1.25.

Euromonitor: International Marketing Data and Statistics, 1994

Fighting the Gulf war cost more than £10 billion a day, and totalled more than 10 times the estimated wealth of the Kuwaiti Investment Fund lodged with British banks.

Estimated total cost of waging the Gulf conflict: $676 billion. Estimated worth of the Kuwaiti Investment Fund on August 3rd 1990: $50 billion.

Panoscope 38/The Arab Monetary Fund/The Times

Market madness: in 24 years, the price of a barrel of crude oil has gone up 50 per cent, while the price of a gallon of 4-star petrol has gone down slightly.

Barrel of crude oil in 1970 at current prices: £6 (75p). In 1994: £9.38. Gallon of 4-star petrol in 1970: £2.60 (33p). In 1994: £2.52.

Department of Trade and Industry, Hansard, vol. 242, no. 93, col. 250

US consumer purchases of electric shavers are set to double in 11 years. (6.2 per cent annual increase)

Predicast Forecasts

US consumer purchases of electric hair dryers are set to double in 11 years. (6.4 per cent annual increase)

Predicast Forecasts

US consumer purchases of electric toasters are set to double in 11 years. (6.4 per cent annual increase)

Predicast Forecasts

US consumer purchases of electric food processors are set to double in 16 years. (4.4 per cent annual increase)

Predicast Forecasts

US consumer purchases of electric can openers are set to double in 11 years. (6.2 per cent annual increase)

Predicast Forecasts

US consumer purchases of electric coffee-makers are set to double in 15 years. (4.5 per cent annual increase)

Predicast Forecasts

US consumer purchases of electric lighted make-up mirrors are set to double in 17 years. (4.1 per cent annual increase)

Predicast Forecasts

The only small energy-consuming appliance US consumers are not buying more of every year is the electric corn-popper.

Predicast Forecasts

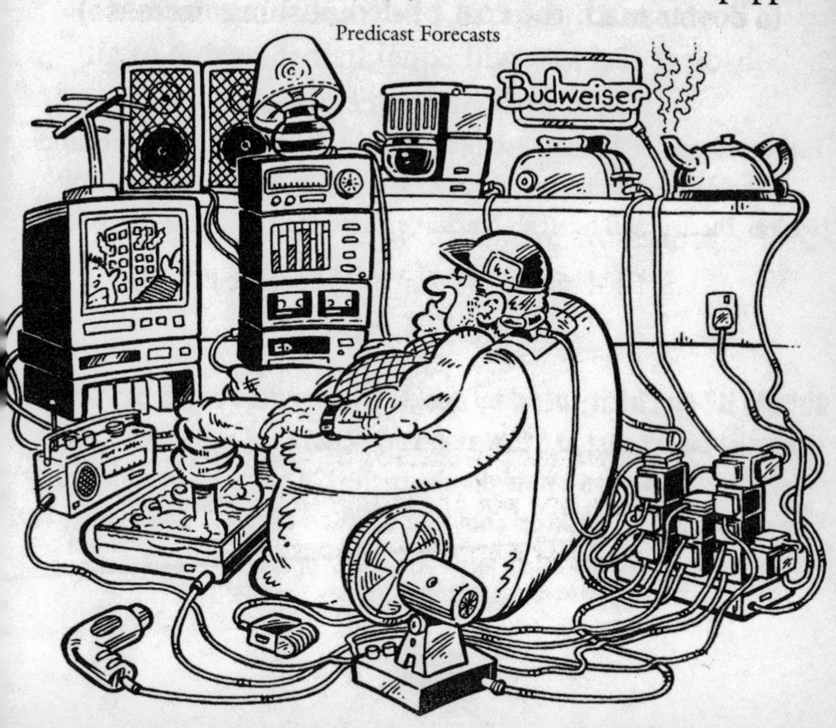

US consumer purchases of vacuum cleaners are set to double in 12 years. (5.8 per cent annual increase)

Predicast Forecasts

Major new electrical appliances bought by American consumers would make 11 stacks as high as Mount Everest every day. (130,000 units averaging 75 cm)

Predicast/Appliance Manufacturer

Power mad: the cost of demolishing today's obsolete reactors will equal half the value of all UK nuclear power plants.

Estimated cost of decommissioning Nuclear Electric's 13 aging reactors assuming no previous accident: £7.8 billion. Current cost value of Nuclear Electric and Scottish Nuclear's tangible fixed assets: £15 billion.

New Scientist 1924/Hansard, vol. 242, no. 97, col. 603

But will it? Electricity used by desktop computers could be halved.

Annual power cost of 120W standard PC: £72. Of energy-efficient model: £30. Annual overnight electricity bill of company with 200 conventional desktop computers left on all night: £22,000.

PC Magazine (Siemens-Nixdorf Green PC (50% on 50% idle, 5.8-99.4w))/
Compaq advertising campaign for Deskpro XL4/66 model

The average American woman owns five pairs of sunglasses.

Business Age, 43

Babies in the richest countries have a 33 times better chance of reaching five years of age than babies born in the poorest countries.

World Health Organisation/British Medical Journal, vol. 310, no. 6989

Santa Claus's sunshine is down by a sixth.

Percentage decrease in Arctic sunshine over the last 40 years due to pollution haze: 15.

New Scientist, no. 1949

The world's whole supertanker fleet would not be able to deliver a year's newspapers to the USA.

Supertanker-loads of newspapers a year recycled by Americans: 230. Dumped: 578. World supertanker fleet: 791. (20.9 & 52.4m short tons, supertanker 100K t)

National Geographic, vol. 186, no. 1/ Department of Transport/John R. Jacobs, World Tanker Fleet Review 1992 (over 100,000 tonnes capacity)

Ninety-six eight-hour days without lunch-breaks would be required to read American anti-pollution regulations.

US Code of Federal Regulations (4 minutes/page)

Far from slowing energy consumption to prevent global warming, Britain is accelerating it.

Million therms of primary fuels and equivalents used in 1991: 89,960. In 1993: 92,307.

Central Statistical Office

Bob dydd fe gy horddir dau lyfr yn y cymraeg.

(Over two books in Welsh are published per working day)

(618 titles in 1993)

The Bookseller, no. 4621

Somebody escapes from a British prison every 38 hours.

Escapers from Welsh and English prisons between 20 June 1988 and 24 March 1994: 1,239.

Hansard, vol. 240, no. 80, col. 941

Britain awards five times more doctorates in technical subjects per year than booming South Korea.

PhDs in Engineering and Tech, Mathematics and Computer Science and Natural Sciences awarded in South Korea in 1990: 685. In the UK: 3,330.

Hansard, vol. 243, no. 102, col. 191

Britain's novels are published at a rate of one every 13 working minutes.

Unitary fiction titles published week of 22 January 1994: 185.

The Bookseller, no. 4597/RM

Women's glossy monthly magazines pay writers about 28 times less for a page than they charge advertisers.

Ratecard cost of page advert in front half of a mid-range glossy magazine: £7,300. Typical non-celebrity writer's pay for a page article: £250.

Media Week 452/RM

50 years from now, the average weekly household fuel and light bill promises to be £500 a week.

Average weekly household fuel and light bill in 1941 was 34p. In 1993: £13.02.

Chronicle of the 20th Century, London, 1988 (6s/5d)/CSO inquiry

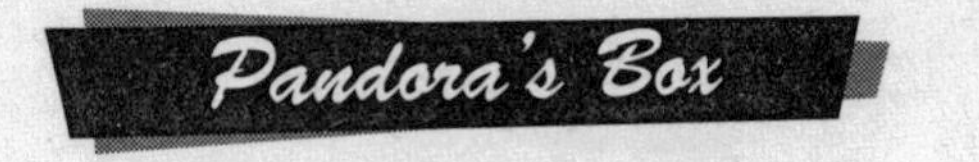

The Beatles' performing fee multiplied by 80 times in one year.

Fee paid by New York impresario to the Beatles for two shows in one day in 1964: $5,500. For one show in 1965: $180,000.

Sid Bernstein, cited in John Glatt, Rage & Roll: Bill Graham and the Selling of Rock, 1993 NY Birch Lane Press.

English girls appear to be twice better taught in the county of Warwickshire than in Leicestershire.

Percentage of schoolgirls getting five or more A–C grade GCSEs in Leicestershire: 30.4. In Warwickshire: 68.4.

Department of Education, School Examinations Survey 1991–92, Hansard, vol. 238, no. 60, col. 806

Japan is expected to hold about 70 tonnes of deadly plutonium within 15 years.

Years' toxic half-life of plutonium's most stable isotope: 25,000.

Atomic Energy Commission/Nature, vol. 369, no. 6482, (69-79t)/The Cambridge Encyclopedia, 1992

America's emerging book supermarkets nearly doubled their sales in a year.

USA book superstore sales in 1992: $526 million. In 1993: $999 million.

The Bookseller, no. 4615

300 Britons go to their graves per biography published.

Minutes of the working day between British publication of a biography: 54. UK deaths per year: 634,000.

The Bookseller, no. 4615/Whitaker's Almanack 1995

Child mortality affects the statistics to make lives in richer countries appear nearly twice as long as those in poorer countries.

Average years' life in a least-developed country: 43.
In a highly developed country: 78.

World Health Organisation/British Medical Journal, vol. 310, no. 6989

Residents of EU countries are 12 times materially better-off than people bordering the south and east Mediterranean. (GDP per capita $1,589/$19,242 in 1992)

Geographical, April 1995

Eight thousand Britons receive their invalidity benefits abroad.

Hansard, vol. 240, no. 80(2), col. 1022

An American dress costs more than a Guatemalan school.

Price tag on a dress in a Melrose Avenue, Los Angeles, boutique: $1,500.

Cost of a communally built schoolhouse in rural Guatemala: $1,200.

L. Baer-Brown & B. Rhein, Earthkeepers, Mercury House USA 1995

The average American's energy use is equivalent to the consumption rate of three Japanese, six Mexicans, 12 Chinese, 33 Indians, 147 Bangladeshis, 281 Tanzanians, or 422 Ethiopians.

L. Baer-Brown & B. Rhein, Earthkeepers, Mercury House USA 1995

Half a century after the end of the British Raj, a quarter of India's rural population still has no safe drinking water.

Percentage of rural population with access to safe drinking water in the former Soviet Union: 100.

Univ of Manchester/Lancet, vol. 345, no. 8957/Information Please Environmental Almanac, 1994

Every working day, British diplomats spend about £27,000 entertaining.

Amount spent by FCO and ODA on entertaining in 1992–3: £6,946,298.

Hansard, vol. 240, no. 80(2), col 1019

Yugoslavian refugees already outnumber Hong Kong British three-to-one.

Former Yugoslavians granted leave to enter the United Kingdom to live 1991–94: 155,900. Hong Kong British citizens granted right of entry after 1997: 50,000.

Home Office, Hansard, vol. 242, no. 93, col. 248/Reuters

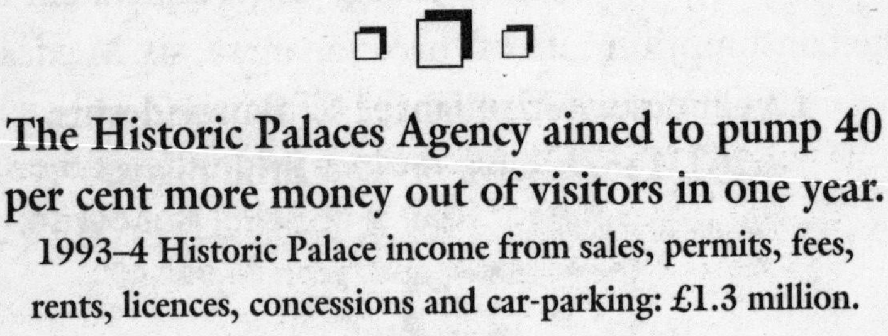

The Historic Palaces Agency aimed to pump 40 per cent more money out of visitors in one year.

1993–4 Historic Palace income from sales, permits, fees, rents, licences, concessions and car-parking: £1.3 million. Target for 1994–5: £1.8 million.

Department of National Heritage, Hansard, vol. 242, no. 97, col. 609

UK forests absorb only one tonne in every 66 of carbon given off by Britons burning fossil fuels.

Sycamore forests covering an area the size of Europe which would be required to absorb 50 years of the world's fossil-fuel carbon dioxide: 1.

(2.5m t per annum, 1.5 per cent of emissions)

New Scientist, no. 1952, 1994/Bill McKibben, The End of Nature, London, 1990

~~WASTE NOT~~

Want Not

A year's discarded motor tyres world-wide could stack 10,000 kilometres into outer space, or 500 times higher than a cruising Concorde.

Motor tyres scrapped each year: 50,000,000

Warmer Bulletin

Demand for difficult-to-recycle polypropylene is set to double in seven years. (10%/yr)

The Engineer, vol. 278, no. 7189/90

Modern rubbish dumps may need 500 years of management by future generations.

The Waste Manager, June 1994

What did they do before? South Koreans' spending on throwaway nappies multiplied seven times in the five years between 1987 and 1992.

Sales of disposable diapers in South Korea in 1987: $22,000,000. In 1992: $163,000,000.

Supertankerloads of wet nappies a year: 1.

Alecia Swasy, Soap Opera, Times Books, 1994, New York

Plastic junked by Americans every year would fill a queue of 158 supertankers stretching 34 miles.

(15.8m USt, 0.4m t recycled, supertanker=100K t, 350 m)

National Geographic, vol. 186, no. 1

Semi-trailer trucks loaded with a day's Bombay rubbish would queue for two miles.

Tons of rubbish produced by Bombay each day: 5,000.

High occupancy of rooms among Bombay's 7 million slum-dwellers: 20–30. (Bombay pop 14m)

BBC News and Current Affairs

More than four supertanker loads of aluminium cans are landfilled or littered in Japan every year.

(435,000 t. in 1989)

Resource Recycling USA

Since the USA's 1965 federal Water Quality Act assured the quality of tapwater, Americans have doubled their soft drink consumption.

Gallons of soft drinks drunk per year by the average American in 1965: 17.8. In 1989: 45.9.

Euromonitor: Consumer USA

A beercan takes 35 times more polluting energy to make than a reusable beer bottle.

BTUs of energy used to make one 12-ounce glass beer bottle: 3,750. One 12-ounce reusable glass beer bottle used 10 times: 200. One 12-ounce aluminium can: 7,000. One 12-ounce steel can: 6,000.

Argonne National Laboratory (USA)

Throwing away a drink can is like tipping away a canful of car fuel.

Canfuls of car fuel (or the energy equivalent) saved by recycling five aluminium cans: 5.

H. Patricia Hynes, Earthright, USA

Making drinks bottles returnable takes 70 to 90 per cent of them off the streets or out of the bin.

The 1994 Information Please Environmental Almanac, USA

In the next minute, rich and successful Hong Kong, with a higher average per capita income than Britain, will dump 60 semi-trailer truck-loads of liquid and solid waste onto its seashore. (2m tonnes per day)

ITN, News At Ten

A year's waste from London, loaded into semi-trailers, could jam up all six lanes of a motorway for over 1,000 miles.

(semi-trailer truck 23t, total 15m tonnes in 1991)

Warmer Bulletin, 41

1,400 UK workers make waste for every one dealing in it.

Weeks it would take semi-trailer trucks loaded with a year's London waste to go by, with one passing every five seconds: 5.

Employment Gazette, vol. 102, no. 10 (19,500 in scrap and waste dealing out of 27.4m)/
Warmer Bulletin, no. 41 (semi-trailer truck 23t, total 15m tonnes in 1991)

Britons burn 437,000 wooden coffins each year, enough to load nearly 1,000 semi-trailer trucks.

Percentage of British wood supplies grown in Britain: 15.

J.B.Bradfield, Green Burial, The Natural Death Centre 1993/
Geographical, October 1994

Swedish law requires households to have at least seven different waste bins (for recycling metals/plastics, paper/cardboard, glass, newspapers, aluminium cans, plastic/glass bottles, rubbish).

Warmer Bulletin, 41

Rubbish-dump scavengers in Recife, Brazil, collect 120 tons of materials a day for recycling.

Warmer Bulletin, 41

Rubbish expands to fill the space available.

Percentage increase in waste volume arising from UK households of three or more when provided with a wheely-bin: 50

Warmer Bulletin, 41, citing MEL Research

About 83 semi-trailer truck-loads of textiles a day are thrown on British rubbish dumps.

Tonnes of clothing and shoes collected at Salvation Army textile banks annually: 24,000. Tonnes of textiles landfilled: 700,000. World refugees: 15 million.

Warmer Bulletin, 41/UN High Comissioner for Refugees

Aerosol cans emerging from UK factories each working day could be littered nose-to-tail from Plymouth to Newcastle.

Years until hair mousse aerosol sales double: 7.4. Until shaving lather aerosols double: 5.

The Grocer (935m in 1993, 20cm each; hair mousse 58m; shaving 93m)/
The Cambridge Encyclopedia

Waste Not Want Not

Nearly all used plastic packaging goes on to the landscape.

Percentage of all UK used plastic consumer packaging that is recycled: 1–2.

Materials Reclamation Weekly

Every day, enough poisonous lead is mined to load a semi-trailer truck jam-up six miles long.

(semi-trailer truck 23t)

Tonnes of lead mined each year world-wide: 5.5 million.

The Lancet, vol. 343, no. 89000

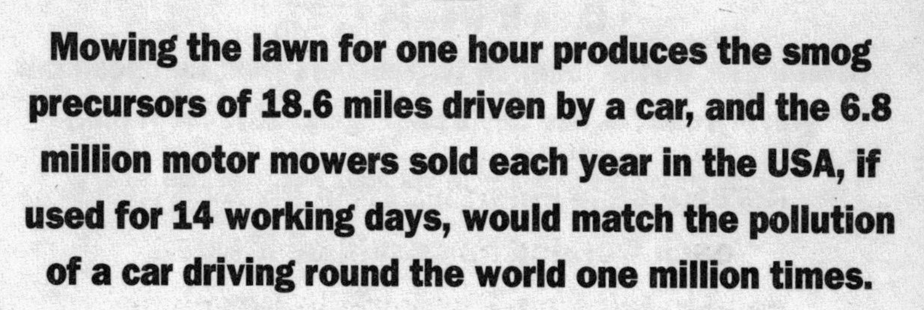

Mowing the lawn for one hour produces the smog precursors of 18.6 miles driven by a car, and the 6.8 million motor mowers sold each year in the USA, if used for 14 working days, would match the pollution of a car driving round the world one million times.

US EPA/New Scientist, no. 1,925/Predicast Forecasts

There's a hole in the ozone layer twice the size of Europe.

Pilkington Barnes Hind contact lens advertisement, March 1995

Water-polluting chemical fertilisers are cheaper now than they were in 1987.

Central Statistical Office, Annual Abstract of Statistics, table 18.4

The equivalent of 328 supertankers of raw or partially treated sewage are tipped into the harbour of Boston, Massachusetts, every day.

Island Press news release 12 August 1991

Pollutant polystyrene is cheaper now than it was in 1987.

Semi-trailer trucks required to transport West European raw polystyrene for one day's packaging: 107. (900t p.a.)

Central Statistical Office, Annual Abstract of Statistics, table 18.4/
British Plastics Federation Statistic Handbook 1990–91

While Washington experts argued over global warming, Americans went out and bought 2.9 million air conditioner units in 1985, and 4.9 million in 1989.

Statistical Abstract of the US, 1993

The last decade of North Sea oil drilling could have left a seabed wasteland of hydrocarbon pollution nearly twice the size of Scotland; or a polluted area the size of Switzerland, Belgium, Holland and Denmark put together.

North Sea oil wells drilled 1983–94: 3,019. Estimated kilometres' diameter of hydrocarbon pollution footprint (oil-based muds and drill cuttings) round an offshore well: 8. (151K sq km)

Department of Trade and Industry, Brown Book 1995/
J. Gray, & F. Olsgard, University of Oslo, cited in New Scientist, no. 1976

2.1 million asthmatics, including about 700,000 children, suck in CFCs with each squeeze of their aerosol-metered inhalers.

Estimated inhalers prescribed annually: 52 million.
(70 per cent of 3m dependants)

3M Airovir

In the next three minutes, a stack of bottles and jars higher than Mount Everest will be dumped on the British isles.

Bottles and jars thrown away annually: 6 billion.
(12-hour day; average 15 cm)

Centre for Alternative Technology, Machynlleth SY20 9AZ

Each of the seven environmental inspectors in Russia's Tyumen oilfield is responsible for an area as big as Wales and England.

Square kilometres of Tyumen oil field: 1 million. Of Wales and England: 150,000.

Prof Alexey Yablokov, Royal Institute of International Affairs

Polluting municipal waste incinerators in Britain encourage five times more waste than in Germany.

Average incineration costs per tonne in the UK: £20. In Germany: £113. Percentage of UK incinerators not complying with EC emission standards to be enforced at end of 1995: 90. Semi-trailer truck-loads of deadly toxic wastes from US armed forces bases reported redistributed into the environment at Rechem, Pontypool: 17. (400 t)

NAWDC, The Waste Manager, June 1994/Hansard, vol. 244, no. 111, col. 151

The world's bloated cattle herd could be causing up to a fifth of a major global-warming gas.

Estimated variable percentage of methane in the atmosphere which comes from cows belching: 7–21.

National Center for Atmospheric Research, USA/New Scientist, no. 1924

Earth's protective ozone layer at the South Pole recently fell to half its historic level.

Normal springtime South Pole concentration of ozone in a column from the ground up through the atmosphere before ozone depletion began: 300. Recorded on 12 October 1993: 91. Percentage reduction in ozone layer March 1995: 50.

Geophysical Research Letters, vol. 21, p. 421/New Scientist, no. 1925 (Dobson Units)/European Stratospheric Arctic and Mid-Latitude Experiment

Shipping away a year of total waste generated by modern Britons would require five times the world fleet of supertankers, or a nose-to-tail queue of semi-trailer trucks stretching six times round the globe. (400m t per annum, semi-trailer truck, 23t)

MAFF

China aims to keep its acid-rain-making sulphur dioxide emissions to 41,000 tonnes a day, or a mere three supertanker-loads a week. (15m t per annum)

Panoscope, no. 39

Every week for four years in the old Moorish town of Cordoba, Spain, the dustmen's haul increased by 200 tonnes.

Cordoba's tonnage of household and commercial rubbish in 1986: 86,000. In 1992: 128,500.

Warmer Bulletin, no. 41 (Cordoba pop. 310,000)

Three out of four new aluminium cans are dumped on the landscape.

Cans littered or sent to landfill in 1994: 5 billion. Recycled: 1.57 billion. Percentage of aluminium cans recycled annually in Britain: 24. In Sweden (with obligatory deposit on cans): 85.

Aluminium Can Recycling Association

Americans bin more than 10 supertanker-loads of paper a week.

Supertanker-loads of paper made in 1990: 771. Recycled or exported for recycling: 220. (70m/20m US tons, supertanker=100K t)

National Geographic, vol. 186, no. 1

Fifty years ago, Americans had more than three times as many recycling projects as they do now.

Community recycling programs among 257 million population: 12,000 (1 per 21,400)

Salvage committees among approximately 130 million population during World War II: 21,000. (1 per 6,200)

National Geographic, vol. 186, no. 1

Heavy publication: semi-trailer trucks delivering a year's requirement of paper for the *National Geographic* magazine would queue nose-to-tail for 22 miles.

(50K USt, semi-trailer truck=23t/50ft)

National Geographic, vol. 186, no. 1

By this time tomorrow, the equivalent of more than 3,000 articulated road-tanker-loads of untreated sewage will have been dumped on Britain's beaches, in effect, a nose-to-tail queue of lorries stretching over 50 kilometres. (22m gal; road-tanker 50ft)

National Rivers Authority

In the next three minutes, a semi-trailer truck-load of plastic will be dumped on the UK landscape.

Tonnes of UK plastic dumped per annum: 2.5 million.

Centre for Alternative Technology, Machynlleth SY20 9AZ (12-hour day)

Water mains in rain-scarce East Anglia lose the equivalent of 57 Olympic swimming pools of fresh water a day. (130m l)

Anglian Water Environmental Report 1994

Laid flat in a row, the US state of Louisiana's littered used tyres could stretch from New Orleans three-quarters of the way round the world.

Estimated number of used tyres strewn about the American state of Louisiana: 40 million. Acres of Louisiana land per tyre: 0.7. (2.5ft/tyre)

Greenwire, 28 June 1991

British Airways staff fly through a freight train of paper a year.

BT Environmental Report, 1994 (800 t; 26 30-tonne wagons)

The number of aluminium beverage cans littered or landfilled every hour of the day and night in the USA would make a stack reaching approximately 350 miles into space, which it would take a barefoot Fijiian 11 days and nights to climb at full speed. (1990, 3.77m)

Alcoa/
Guinness Book of Records

Jet planes use nearly a third as much fuel as all other petrol-powered engines, without taxation.

Articulated road-tankers of inland petrol used in the UK per year: 792,000. Of aviation turbine fuel: 237,000.

Taxation on aviation fuel: £0.

Central Statistical Office, Monthly Digest of Statistics, no. 589

Nine supertankers a week would be required to ship away the packaging wasted by Americans.

Tons of US packaging waste in 1990: 47.4 million.

Proportion of all rubbish: 1/3.

The Coalition of Northeast Governors, Greenwire 22 December 1993 (1990)

A year's worth of Europe's junked aerosol cans could easily stack to the Moon.

Aerosol cans thrown away unrecycled every year: 2.55 billion.

Kilometres high when stacked: 408,000.

Moon's average kilometre distance: 382,000.

Aerosols: Recycling & Disposal, BAMA (aerosol 16 cm)/
The Cambridge Concise Encyclopedia 1992

Russia's environmental disaster areas are nearly 20 times bigger – no, not than England's – than England.

Square kilometres of Russian disaster zones: 2.55 million. (15 per cent)

Square kilometres of England: 130,000.

Russian Ministry of the Environment/Reuters

In the next seven days, British civilization will emit the equivalent of 31 supertanker loads of liquefied, global-warming carbon dioxide.

House of Commons Official Report, vol. 256, no. 68, (750m t CO2 to 2000)

Approximately 10,000 silk worms are boiled alive to make a single silk garment.

M. Tobias, Environmental Meditation: 1993 Freedom, USA

Far from being reduced, UK domestic electricity consumption is on a steady course to double over the lifetime of 11 Parliaments.

Number of stacks as high as the Blackpool Tower of colour TVs sold on one day could make: 27.

MarketLine International (1.5 per cent/yr to 109.1 TWh in 2000)/
Euromonitor: Consumer Europe, 1995 (9,452 @ 18" high)

World oil consumption would empty Britain's remaining proven reserves in 274 days.

UK Millions of tonnes proven oil reserves: 2,360. World tonnage used per day: 8,582,000.

Department of Trade and Industry Brown Book (end of 1994)/BP plc (1991)

Germany spends four times more organizing the recycling of all waste than Britain spends collecting and dumping domestic rubbish.

1994 cost of Duales System Deutschland: £1.6 billion. UK controlled domestic rubbish disposal cost: £350 million. (15 per cent of 137m tonnes @ average £17/t)

Warmer Bulletin

Americans recycle enough steel in a year to build seven supertankers, and dump enough to build – wait for it – another 38.

(10.4m & 1.9m US tons; supertanker=300K t)

National Geographic, vol. 186, no. 1

About 500 semi-trailer truck-loads of consumer appliance batteries are thrown onto the landscape every year.

Percentage of 460 million retailed battery cells recycled annually: 0. (1993, 11,500 tonnes, 25gm average)

The Cadmium Association/The Grocer, citing MINTEL

Every day, Americans use a quantity of paper that requires over three million trees to make.

L. Baer-Brown & B. Rhein, Earthkeepers, Mercury House USA, 1995

Building a typical American dream-home generates seven tons of construction rubbish.

Number of supertankers that UK unrecycled construction site waste would fill every year: 260.

Worldwatch Institute Paper 124/Warmer Bulletin, no. 45

In the next three seconds, sufficient cans to build a 26-storey high stack will be dumped on the British landscape.

(12-hour day; 2,260 11cm cans)

Cans dumped per annum by Britons: 11.9 billion.

Centre for Alternative Technology, Machynlleth SY20 9AZ

Imports of coal and gas have multiplied 21 times in 10 years.

Coal and gas imports by 1,000 tonnes of oil equivalent in 1983: 480. In 1993: 10,390.

Department of Trade and Industry, Hansard, vol. 248, no. 143

Nuclear reactor electricity now exceeds the amount of electricity available throughout the world in 1958.

Average years' life of the 81 reactors taken out of service: 17.

International Atomic Energy Agency/L. Brown, et al, Vital Signs, London 1994

A day's German steel production could build 22 Eiffel Towers.

Quid, Laffont Paris 1992/Euromonitor

A 1,000-mile line-up of semi-trailer trucks would be required to truck away a year's tonnage of sulphur dioxide and nitrogen dioxide emitted from Wales' and England's power stations.

Percentage of streetlights that stay on all night: 98.

(2,446K t in 1993)

House of Commons Official Report, vol. 256, no. 71, col. 538/
British Astronomical Association/New Scientist, no. 1969

The USA could be 70 per cent dependent on imported oil by the year 2010.

Months it would take an oil-less USA to suck dry every oil tanker in the world: 7.

US Dept of Energy's Energy Information Administration (#18)/
Greenwire 08.29.91/Euromonitor International Marketing Data and Statistics 1994 (606m t in 1990)/DoT/John R. Jacobs, World Tanker Fleet Review, 1992 (total tanker fleet capacity: c.360m tonnes)

The British Isles are surrounded by an estimated 100,000 shipwrecks, or one every day for the last 273 years.

BBC Radio 4, Going Places

Since warnings of global warming and climate damage spread in the early 1980s, British consumers have increased their annual spending on global-warming purchases such as electricity, gas, major electrical appliances, motor vehicles, petrol/oil and air travel by over 30 per cent, or £14 billion a year.

Central Statistical Office, Annual Abstract of Statistics, table 14.10 (1983–93 at constant 1990 prices)

Europe alone could empty the oil reserves of the United Arab Emirates in 12 years; the world could empty them in fewer than four.

Supertankers of oil used per year in Europe: 10,700. In the world: 35,390. In reserve in the United Arab Emirates: 129,000.

Euromonitor European Marketing Data and Statistics, 1994 (1,070m t)/ Allan M Findless, The Arab World, 1994 Routledge (12,900m t; 35,390m t; supertanker 100K t)

America's publicly owned Allegheny National Forest contains within its boundaries so many private oil and gas wells that they are estimated to number 14,000.

Philadelphia Inquirer

138,495 Americans were shot by children under six years old in the 1980s.

Harpers magazine (1981–91, citing US General Accounting Office 19 March 1991, extrapolated by 1:105 fatal/non-fatal accident ratio from 1,319 fatal shootings)

In the eighteenth century, Rome had nearly 200 times London's murder conviction rate.

Murder convictions in London and Middlesex 1749–71: 81.
In half that period in Rome: 4,000.
(Rome 1/4 London's population)

V.A.C. Gatrell, The Hanging Tree, OUP 1994

Fighting World War II today would cost the British state four times its total annual budget each year.

Daily cost of World War II: £11 million. Number of times the UK state budget exceeds that of 1939: 250. Spent on war in 1993-94: £21.5 billion. Jobs in industry sustained by war expenditure 1992-93: 425,000.

Chronicle of the 20th Century, London 1988/
Ministry of Defence House of Commons Official Report, vol. 251, no. 25

Government trade and industry officials spend more than £14,000 a day on telephone calls.

Department of Trade and Industry House of Commons Official Report, vol. 251, no. 25

Employees in UK mechanical engineering, office machinery, electrical engineering and instruments have nearly halved since 1971.

(2.1m in 1971 to 1.2m in 1993)

Employment Gazette, vol. 102, no. 10

Placed end-to-end, trees felled by humans worldwide during a Xmas–New Year holiday season would easily stretch to the Moon.

(35m, average length 40ft)

Greenwire

Britons work 72 million hours less per week than they did in 1989.

Hours worked per week in summer 1994 by employees and self-employed: 813 million. In spring 1989: 885 million.

Department of Employment, House of Commons Official Report, vol. 251, no. 25

In modern Britain more than one in 10 mature, experienced males in their 50s are unemployed.

Percentage of British males aged 50-59 unemployed: 8.4. Females: 4.7.

Department of Employment, House of Commons Official Report, vol. 251, no. 25

Business property tax payable by the Crown Inn, Woolhope, England in 1994–95: £1,780. In 1995–96: £13,521.

Peter Temple-Morris MP, House of Commons Official Report, vol. 257, no. 78, col. 671

Tomorrow, 22 million steel cans will be dumped on the British Isles.

The Grocer

The US Department of Energy's nuclear waste could fill 23 football fields 10 feet deep.

John Fleck, Albuquerque Journal

131,578 residents of sunny Florida make 150,000 tons of rubbish in one year; it takes 312,500 people in Tokyo or 882,352 in Cairo to match them.

Greenwire

All the tankers in the world together could not ship away a year's Western European waste.

Tonnes of domestic, industrial and hazardous waste produced by EU countries in a year: 382.4 million. Total world tanker tonnage capacity: 360 million.

Euromonitor European Marketing Data and Statistics 1994/
John R. Jacobs, World Tanker Fleet Review 1992

The city of Los Angeles sends five semi-trailer trucks a week of reject junk mail to the dump.

Percentage of Los Angeles landfills which is junk mail: 3.

Los Angeles Times

If all the toxic soil of the US military's Rocky Mountain Arsenal were dumped in a ditch three feet deep and three feet wide, it would stretch from Denver to China.

Conservation International

The USA's science budget is 36 times bigger than Britain's.

Britain's overall science budget 1995–96: $2 billion.
The USA's proposed science budget for the same year: $73bn.

New Scientist, no. 1964/Nature, vol. 373, no. 6514

American viewers watch 3.5 million years worth of TV commercials per year, Britons about 700,000 years worth. (USA 30.6bn hours)

Earth Island Journal

Over a quarter of a million English pupils attend a state secondary school class numbering more than 36 pupils.

Deptartment of Education, House of Commons Official Report, vol. 251, no. 25

Every working day, France spends more than four times as much public money on the arts as Britain.

The UK's arts spending per working day: £964,000. France's: £3.8 million.

Sunday Times, 11 June 1994/Quid, Robert Laffont, Paris (Arts Council £187m, until April 1997; UK business £69.5m)

Half of London's premier walk-through culture facilities had lower attendances in 1991 than in 1981.

Science Museum visitors in 1981: 3,486,228. In 1991: 1,327,503.

Imperial War Museum visitors in 1981: 796,000. In 1991: 338,301.

Central Statistical Office Annual Abstract of Greater London Statistics, vol. 24

Canada spends more than half as much again on education as Britain.

Percentage of its gross domestic product spent on education by Britain: 4.7. By Canada: 7.2.

Department of Education, University of Southampton

Under 17 per cent of all first-run broadcast TV fiction series are created by women.

(1991 to mid-1995 overall in the UK)

Broadcast, 24 March 1995

Sales of surplus war equipment could provide five new writers' bursaries a working hour, supporting more than 10,000 authors a year.

Current number of £7,000 writers' bursaries granted by the Arts Council of England: 15. (£72.4m/yr)

House of Commons Official Report, vol. 265, no. 68, col. 254/Arts Council of England

An American child may be watching as many as 19,500 violent acts a year on television.

Average number of acts of violence depicted per hour per channel on a day's TV in the USA in 1994: 15. In 1992: 10. (25 hrs/wk)

Variety, 8–14 August 1994

Cockroaches can run towards a tourist at the human equivalent of 200 mph.

Average number of cockroaches per apartment surveyed near the University of Florida: 80,000.

Focus magazine

One Sainsbury supermarket is supplied by an average of 32 meat farms.

The Grocer, vol. 217, no. 7204

The 1995 draught Guinness marketing budget could have stood every male British drinker a free pint.

Guinness sales budget: £35 million. Cost of 18 million pints of draught Guinness: £34.2 million. (@ £1.90/pint)

The Grocer

One gram of northern forest soil contains up to 5,000 species, almost all of them unknown to science.

Edward O. Wilson/American Association for the Advancement of Science

Spanish conquerors found 136,000 sacrificial human skulls beneath the temple of Queztlcoatl in Mexico City.

Student Outlook, 10

Today, the Saudi Arabian royal family will spend more than £12 million on its personal requirements.

S. Aburish, The Rise, Corruption and Coming Fall of the House of Saud, London, 1994

The combined weight of all Earth's insects is 12 times that of the human race.

Estimated number of spiders and insects: 5 million billion.

R. Ash, The Top Ten of Everything, Dorling Kindersley, 1994

It takes nearly four supertanker loads of grain to raise Chinese annual beer consumption by one bottle per adult. (370,000t)

Lester B. Brown, State of the World 1995, Earthscan

The average UK passport-checking officer takes aside only one incoming person per two weeks.

Passport-holders subject to 'further examination' in 1993: 63,000.
Ports (and airports) directorate passport staff: 2,425. Entry Into The UK, London, HMSO

US state executioners could kill a prisoner once a working hour for a year and a half.

Number of persons awaiting execution in the USA: 3,000.

Average years' wait for execution: 7.

Amnesty magazine

Tonight more than 1,000 UK small businesses will be burgled.

Small businesses burgled in 1994: 400,000.

The Forum of Private Business/The Grocer

Over half a million Britons have been prosecuted for cannabis offences in the last 25 years.

Deaths known to have been caused in 1990 by use of illegal cannabis: 0. By use of legal tobacco: 110,000.

National Youth Agency/Home Office, cited in New Scientist

If customs are seizing 10 per cent of all cocaine imported, it follows that cocaine dealers are evading taxes on retail sales of nearly £1 billion a year.

Grams of of cocaine seized on an average working day by the customs in 1994: 8,480.

Average retail cost of a gram of cocaine: £40.

HM Customs & Excise/Sunday Times

Every day, 68 Americans commit murder.

Homicides expected in the USA each year: 25,000.

Amnesty International

Fishing trawlers kill on average 16lb of marine life for every 1lb taken to market.

World At One, BBC Radio 4

Two supertanker-loads of refined sugar a year are added to UK processed foods.

Spoonfuls of sugar contained in a large cola soft-drink: 21.

Nature, vol. 373, no. 6514/The Full Treatment (programme supplement), Thames TV, 1992 (200K t)

A drivers' shopping centre proposed for fields near Stow-on-the-Wold is more than one-quarter the size of the English market town.

Britons without a driving licence: 28.2 million.

Geoffrey Clifton-Brown MP, House of Commons Official Report, vol. 256, no. 71/Department of Transport

Nearly 10 per cent of the cost of all UK imports is food and 15 per cent of UK farmland is in set-aside.

Central Statistical Office, Annual Abstract of Statistics 1995/Farmers Weekly

Over the last 20 years, the spreading of more than 50 nerve-gas-based insecticide and herbicide compounds on the Canadian prairie has doubled.

Geographical, June 1995

A year's junked razors could follow the white line along all Britain's trunk roads.

Razors thrown away every year: 185 million.

(£130m market, unit cost 7p; length 10cm)

The Grocer, vol. 217, no. 7204/Whitaker's Almanack 1995 (11,500 m)

Every day, Britons spread two supertanker loads of chemical fertilizers, and still spend over £8.5 million on foreign fruit and vegetables. (70m t/yr)

Central Statistical Office, Annual Abstract of Statistics, 1995

American farmers use the weight of seven World Trade Centers of pesticides a year.

(465m lb in 1990, 650m lb in 1976) (Trade Center – 290K t)

US Council on Environmental Quality Annual Report/Quid 1995 Robert Laffont

Only one in 300 of the world's head of cattle are threatened by BSE and they are virtually all British cattle treated with pesticides.

Head of cattle on Earth: 1,300,000,000. Number of UK cows: 4,340,688. Cattle BSE prediction for 1994: 11,000.

J. Rifkin, Beyond Beef, New York, 1993/MAFF/
Welsh office, Hansard, vol. 263, no. 133 (Wales/England)

British women flush at least two billion items of sanitary protection towards rivers and beaches every year.

Semi-trailer truck-loads of plastic items flushed down UK toilets every year: 2,434. (56,000t)

The Waste Manager

Nearly half of Britain's coastline is polluted with sewage and consumer waste.

Percentage of beaches considered to be in 'excellent' condition: 8. Olympic swimming pools of untreated sewage emitted annually onto Britain's coasts: 144,000. (200m+ galls per diem)

Norwich Union Beachwater inspection/
Geographical, March 1995/National Rivers Authority

Oil rigs in the Gulf of Mexico have spread drilling waste over a seabed area bigger than Wales and England.

Kilometre radius of drilling waste and oil pollution round North Sea oil rigs: 4. Platforms in the Gulf of Mexico: 3,100.

J. Gray & F. Olsgard, University of Oslo, cited in New Scientist, no, 1976/Quid 1995, Paris, Robert Laffont

Every day, more than five new industrial chemicals are added to the estimated 150,000 already polluting the oceans.

Enviromental Investigation Agency (Dr Kevin Brown, Durham University)

Each priest resigning as a result of women's ordination is expected to cost the Church of England about £140,000.

House of Commons Official Report, vol. 356, no. 69, col. 357

In six years, oil companies dumped eight supertanker-loads of polluted oil-well tailings on the bed of the North Sea. (8 x 100K t, 1984-90)

J. Gray & F. Olsgard, University of Oslo, cited in New Scientist, no, 1976

Up to 70 times more is spent promoting baby formula than promoting breast-feeding.

Annual spending per UK baby of the manufactured baby milk industry: £6.40. Of the Government breast-feeding promotion programme: 9p–20p.

Alex Carlile MP, House of Commons Official Report, vol. 257, no. 76, col. 315

There are nearly three times more births out of wedlock now than when Britain was at war and occupied by wealthy young American troops.

Percentage of all maternities conceived out of wedlock in 1944: 12.3. In the 1990s: 32.

David Reynolds, Rich Relations, Harper Collins 1995/
William Davis, The Lucky Generation, Headline, 1994

Almost a third of the petrol that goes through a two-stroke outboard motor is spewed into the water.

National Geographic, vol. 187, no. 5

Buying foreign factory-made goods costs the equivalent of £1,884 a year per British adult.

CSO Annual Abstract of Statistics table 12.4 (1992)

Women do better in Iraq's palaces than in Britain's.

Number of the 270 members elected to Iraq's majlis legislature in 1992 who are women: 3. Of the Queen's senior household staff who are: 0. (heads and deputies of all offices and departments sexable by name)

J. Simpson, Lifting The Veil, Hodder & Stoughton, 1995/ Whitaker's Almanack 1994

The major privatisations have involved an expropriation of more than £323 from every British adult. (£16.8bn debts written off 1980-95, figures unadjusted)

House of Commons Official Report, vol. 257, no. 77, col. 287

A rail trip by a member of the royal family costs 6,300 times more than a similar journey by a member of the public.

Average cost of a journey by royals: £19,101. By a member of the public in normal railcars: £3.00. (45 trips in 1994/£2m allocated 1995–96)

Dept of Transport, House of Commons Official Report, 31 March/BR press office (1993–4)

About 10 million aluminium cans are littered or dumped every day by Britons – a stack about 200 times higher than Mount Everest

Elkington and Hailes, The Green Consumer Guide

Britons use enough energy-intensive aluminium drink cans in a year to stretch end-to-end round the world 26 times. (7bn)

Elkington and Hailes, The Green Consumer Guide

A thrown-away aluminium can could have cost 80 times its weight in global-warming carbon dioxide.

Pounds of carbon dioxide emitted to produce one once-used aluminium can with coal-generated electricity: 5.

Information Please Environmental Almanac (USA)

In spite of recycling efforts, nearly four million aluminium drinks cans per hour are sprayed over the American landscape day and night.

Aluminum beverage cans littered or landfilled annually in the USA: 33,000,000,000.

Alcoa

Americans discard enough aluminium to rebuild all their air force aircraft every three months.

Aluminum drinks cans claimed to be recycled annually in the USA: 55 billion.

Bulletin of Atomic Scientists (USA)/Alcoa (1990)

Mexicans are champion Coca-Cola drinkers at 306 8oz servings of the flavoured sugar-water concoction per person, the British are at one-third their level with 95 and the people of India trail last at nil.

The Coca Cola Company

Americans drink one million gallons of soft drinks an hour round the clock, or the contents of an Olympic swimming pool disappearing with a sucking noise every 30 minutes.

In Context magazine

Index

Index

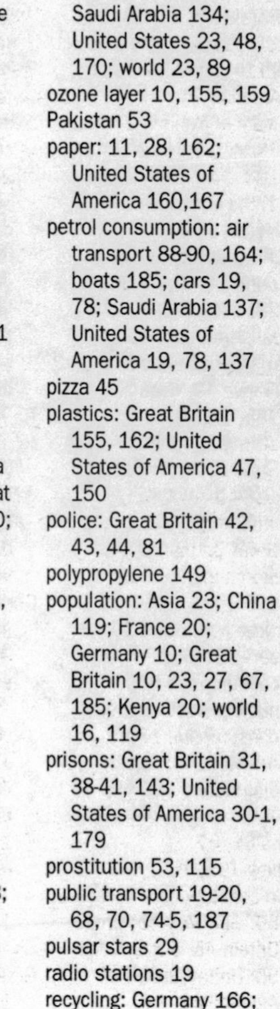